U.S. BUSINESS TAX SYSTEM AND GLOBAL COMPETIVENESS

U.S. BUSINESS TAX SYSTEM AND GLOBAL COMPETIVENESS

RAYMOND E. CARLE

Nova Science Publishers, Inc.
New York

Copyright © 2009 by Nova Science Publishers, Inc.

All rights reserved. No part of this book may be reproduced, stored in a retrieval system or transmitted in any form or by any means: electronic, electrostatic, magnetic, tape, mechanical photocopying, recording or otherwise without the written permission of the Publisher.

For permission to use material from this book please contact us:
Telephone 631-231-7269; Fax 631-231-8175
Web Site: http://www.novapublishers.com

NOTICE TO THE READER

The Publisher has taken reasonable care in the preparation of this book, but makes no expressed or implied warranty of any kind and assumes no responsibility for any errors or omissions. No liability is assumed for incidental or consequential damages in connection with or arising out of information contained in this book. The Publisher shall not be liable for any special, consequential, or exemplary damages resulting, in whole or in part, from the readers' use of, or reliance upon, this material.

Independent verification should be sought for any data, advice or recommendations contained in this book. In addition, no responsibility is assumed by the publisher for any injury and/or damage to persons or property arising from any methods, products, instructions, ideas or otherwise contained in this publication.

This publication is designed to provide accurate and authoritative information with regard to the subject matter covered herein. It is sold with the clear understanding that the Publisher is not engaged in rendering legal or any other professional services. If legal or any other expert assistance is required, the services of a competent person should be sought. FROM A DECLARATION OF PARTICIPANTS JOINTLY ADOPTED BY A COMMITTEE OF THE AMERICAN BAR ASSOCIATION AND A COMMITTEE OF PUBLISHERS.

LIBRARY OF CONGRESS CATALOGING-IN-PUBLICATION DATA

Available upon request.

ISBN: 978-1-60692-255-2

Published by Nova Science Publishers, Inc. ✛ New York

CONTENTS

Preface		**vii**
Executive Summary		**1**
Chapter 1	The U.S. Business Tax System Presents Challenges to U.S. Competitiveness	**5**
Chapter 2	Replacing Business Income Taxes with a Business Activities Tax	**27**
Chapter 3	Business Tax Reform with Base Broadening/ Reform of the U.S. International Tax Rules	**57**
Chapter 4	Addressing Structural Problems with the U.S. Business Tax System	**85**
Index		**147**

PREFACE

The global economy has changed markedly over the past half century. Trade and investment flow across borders in greater volume and with greater ease. Increasingly, the ability of U.S. companies to grow and prosper depends on their ability to do business globally.

As we look to the future of the U.S. economy and U.S. workers, we must look at our competitiveness through the lens of the global marketplace. There are many factors that affect the ability of U.S. workers and U.S. companies to compete globally, and issues as diverse as education, immigration, and trade policy have all been examined in this context. This book examines the role of tax policy in affecting the global competitiveness of U.S. companies and U.S. workers. This is an edited and excerpted edition.

Chapter 1 - Americans deserve a tax system that is simple, fair, and pro-growth – in tune with the nation's dynamic economy. The tax relief proposed by President Bush and enacted by Congress in the past few years has helped lay the foundation for considering ways to ensure that the U.S. tax system helps U.S. businesses compete in a global economy. In 2005, the President established the President's Advisory Panel on Federal Tax Reform (the Tax Panel) to identify the major problems with the current tax system and to provide recommendations on making the tax code simpler, fairer, and better suited to the modern economy. The Tax Panel's report recommended two options for comprehensive overhaul of our federal income tax system – the Growth and Investment Tax plan and the Simplified Income Tax plan. These approaches differ somewhat, but both would reduce taxes on business and capital income.

Chapter 2 - This chapter examines replacing present U.S. business income taxes with a broad- based Business Activities Tax (BAT), which is a type of consumption tax. Assuming a very broad base, a BAT imposed at a rate of roughly 5 percent to 6 percent would replace the revenue from current U.S. business income taxes.

Chapter 3 - The existing U.S. system of taxing capital income creates a number of distortions that interfere with the efficient and productive functioning of the U.S. economy. These distortions include: a tax disincentive to save and invest generally, caused by taxing the return earned on investment; a tax disincentive to invest in the corporate business sector, caused by the double tax on corporate profits; a tax incentive for corporations to finance with debt rather than with equity, caused by tax provisions that allow firms to deduct interest but not dividends; a tax incentive to engage in certain economic activities rather than others, caused by special tax provisions that are only selectively available; and a tax disincentive to repatriating foreign earnings. These distortions waste economic resources and lower the standard of living produced by the U.S. economy.

This chapter discusses approaches for reform of business income taxation that would broaden the tax base and either lower the business tax rate or provide a faster write-off of the cost of investment. It also discusses an approach for reforming the U.S. international tax system by moving to a territorial tax system.

Chapter 4 - In contrast with the previous chapters, this chapter considers several approaches that address specific areas of business income taxation that could be reformed separately or in the context of broad-based reform. A comprehensive approach, however, is likely to be more effective in improving the competitiveness of the U.S. business tax system than addressing specific issues outside of broad-based business tax reform. These approaches are presented as part of a fully informed public policy discussion.

EXECUTIVE SUMMARY

The global economy has changed markedly over the past half century. Trade and investment flow across borders in greater volume and with greater ease. Increasingly, the ability of U.S. companies to grow and prosper depends on their ability to do business globally.

As we look to the future of the U.S. economy and U.S. workers, we must look at our competitiveness through the lens of the global marketplace. There are many factors that affect the ability of U.S. workers and U.S. companies to compete globally, and issues as diverse as education, immigration, and trade policy have all been examined in this context. This paper examines the role of tax policy in affecting the global competitiveness of U.S. companies and U.S. workers.

In the 1960s, international trade and investment flows were much less important to the U.S. economy and the decisions of U.S. companies than they are today. Thus, the United States was free to make decisions about its tax system based primarily on domestic considerations. Moreover, our trading partners generally followed the U.S. lead in tax policy.

Globalization – the growing interdependence of countries resulting from increasing integration of trade, finance, investment, people, information, and ideas in one global marketplace – has resulted in increased cross-border trade and the establishment of production facilities and distribution networks around the globe. Businesses now operate more freely across borders, and business location and investment decisions are more sensitive to tax considerations than in the past.

As barriers to cross-border movement of capital and goods have been reduced, differences in nations' tax systems have become a greater factor in the success of global companies. Recognizing this, many nations have changed their business tax systems. During the past two decades, many of our major trading partners have lowered their corporate tax rates, some dramatically. The United States, which had a low corporate tax rate in the late 1980s as compared to other countries in the Organisation for Economic Co-operation and Development (OECD), now has the second highest statutory corporate tax rate among OECD countries. Moreover, other OECD countries continue to reduce their corporate income tax rates leaving the United States further behind.

As other nations modernize their business tax systems to recognize the realities of the global economy, U.S. companies increasingly suffer a competitive disadvantage. The U.S. business tax system imposes a burden on U.S. companies and U.S. workers by raising the cost of investment in the United States and burdening U.S. firms as they compete with other firms in foreign markets.

Taxing business income discourages investment by raising the cost of capital. The higher the cost of capital, the greater the disincentive to invest. The relatively high U.S. tax rate, compared to our trading partners, places a higher cost on investment. Business taxes play a particularly key role in the economy because they influence the incentive to acquire and use capital – the plants, offices, equipment, and software that corporations employ to produce goods and services. In general, an economy with more capital is more productive and ultimately attains a higher standard of living than economies that have accumulated less capital. Workers gain when businesses have more capital and, correspondingly, workers stand to lose when the tax system leads businesses to invest less and have a smaller capital stock.

On July 26, 2007, the Treasury Department hosted a conference on *Global Competitiveness and Business Tax Reform* that brought together distinguished leaders and experts to discuss how the U.S. business tax system could be improved to make U.S. businesses more competitive. The conference highlighted the need for the U.S. business tax system to be reformed to keep pace with the changing global economy and the changes in the business tax systems of other nations.

This chapter is a follow-up to the July 26th conference and, as with the conference, it seeks to advance an important dialogue on the key linkages between tax policy and American competitiveness in the global economy. Three broad approaches for reforming the U.S. business tax system are outlined: (1) replacing business income taxes with a business activities tax (BAT), a type of consumption tax, (2) eliminating special business tax provisions coupled with either business tax rate reduction or faster write-off of business investment, potentially combined with the exemption of active foreign earnings, and (3) implementing specific changes that focus on important structural problems within our business tax system. Rather than present a particular recommendation, this chapter examines the strengths and weaknesses of the various approaches. The various policy ideas discussed in this chapter represent just some of the approaches that could be considered. This chapter does not advocate any specific recommendation nor does it call for or advance any legislative package or regulatory changes.

The approaches discussed in this chapter would improve the competitiveness of the United States as compared to the current system for taxing U.S. businesses.

Nevertheless, the approaches differ in a number of dimensions. The BAT described in Chapter II would possibly provide the largest benefit in terms of its effect on expanding the size of the economy – ultimately increasing output by roughly 2.0 percent to 2.5 percent – but raises a number of serious implementation and administrative issues.

Chapter III discusses base broadening, which could entail elimination of certain business tax provisions that make substantial contributions to economic growth, such as accelerated deprecation. Thus their elimination may offset some of the economic benefits of business tax rate reduction. While dramatically broadening the business tax base could finance a reduction of the business tax rate to 28 percent, retaining accelerated depreciation and maintaining revenue neutrality would only lower the business tax rate to 31 percent. Alternatively, base broadening and faster write-off of business investment (i.e., 35-percent expensing) would have a substantial effect on the size of the economy – ultimately increasing output by roughly 1.5 percent – but would have effects that may vary considerably across industries and sectors. Chapter III also discusses international taxation and considers issues regarding territorial tax systems.

Chapter IV focuses on specific areas of business income taxation that could be reformed separately or in the context of a broad-based reform. These include, for example, the multiple taxation of corporate profits, the tax bias favoring debt finance, the tax treatment of losses, and book-tax conformity. A comprehensive approach, however, is likely to be more effective in improving the competitiveness of the U.S. business tax system than addressing specific issues outside of broad-based business tax reform.

A fundamental question is the extent to which any of these approaches would markedly affect the competitiveness of U.S. businesses. Lowering the business tax rate to 31 percent would mean that instead of having the second highest statutory corporate tax rate among the thirty OECD countries, the United States would have the third highest tax rate, while with a 28-percent U.S. statutory corporate tax rate, the United States would have the fifth highest tax rate. Providing faster write-off of investment, either through partial expensing or replacing business income taxes with a BAT, may provide larger economic benefits, but would take the United States in a different policy direction.

Moreover, today's global landscape continues to shift as other countries contemplate further changes in their business tax systems. Thus, it remains unclear whether a revenue neutral reform would provide a reduction in business taxes sufficient to enhance the competitiveness of U.S. businesses.

In summary, because the role of the United States in the world economy is changing, because business taxes play an important role in economic decision-making by influencing the incentive to acquire and use capital, and because foreign competitors are reforming their business tax systems, now is the time for the United States to re-evaluate its business tax system to ensure that U.S. businesses and U.S. workers are as competitive as possible and Americans continue to enjoy rising living standards.

Chapter 1

THE U.S. BUSINESS TAX SYSTEM PRESENTS CHALLENGES TO U.S. COMPETITIVENESS

A. INTRODUCTION

Americans deserve a tax system that is simple, fair, and pro-growth – in tune with the nation's dynamic economy. The tax relief proposed by President Bush and enacted by Congress in the past few years has helped lay the foundation for considering ways to ensure that the U.S. tax system helps U.S. businesses compete in a global economy. In 2005, the President established the President's Advisory Panel on Federal Tax Reform (the Tax Panel) to identify the major problems with the current tax system and to provide recommendations on making the tax code simpler, fairer, and better suited to the modern economy. The Tax Panel's report recommended two options for comprehensive overhaul of our federal income tax system – the Growth and Investment Tax plan and the Simplified Income Tax plan.[1] These approaches differ somewhat, but both would reduce taxes on business and capital income.

In 2007, Secretary Paulson initiated a review of the nation's system for taxing businesses. On July 26, 2007, the Secretary hosted a conference on *Global Competitiveness and Business Tax Reform*, at which distinguished leaders and experts discussed how the current business tax system can be improved to make U.S. businesses more competitive in today's global economy. The conference highlighted the need for reform. The participants stressed that the business tax system has not kept pace with changes in the world economy. The United States has become increasingly linked to the world economy through trade and investment. Businesses operate more freely across borders and business location and investment decisions are more sensitive to tax considerations than in the past. Several countries have responded to the increasingly competitive environment by reforming their corporate incomes taxes and reducing corporate income tax rates. The conference participants expressed a conviction that in order for U.S. companies and U.S. workers to compete and thrive in today's global economic climate, the U.S. business tax system also must adapt to these changes.

The discussion at the conference emphasized that the global economy is very different today than it was in the 1 960s, the time when many of our current tax rules regarding cross-border activities and investment were first enacted. The same is true of the U.S. role in the global economy. In the 1960s, international trade and investment flows were much less important to the U.S. economy than they are today. Thus, the United States was free to make decisions about its tax system based primarily on domestic considerations. Moreover, U.S. trading partners generally followed the U.S. lead in tax policy.

Circumstances have changed. Globalization – the growing interdependence of countries resulting from increasing integration of trade, finance, investment, people, information, and ideas in one global marketplace – has resulted in increased cross-border trade and the establishment of production facilities and distribution networks around the globe. Technology continues to accelerate the growth of the worldwide marketplace for goods and services. Advances in communications, information technology, and transport have dramatically reduced the cost and time required to move goods, capital, people, and information around the world. Firms in the global marketplace differentiate themselves by applying more cost-efficient technologies or innovating faster than their competitors.

The significance of globalization to the U.S. economy is apparent from the statistics on international trade and investment. In 1960, trade in goods to and from the United States represented just over 6 percent of Gross Domestic Product (GDP). Today, it represents over 20 percent of GDP, a three-fold increase, while trade in goods and services amounts to more than 25 percent of GDP.[2]

Cross-border investment, both inflows and outflows, also has grown dramatically since 1960. Cross-border investment represented just over 1 percent of GDP in 1960, but by 2006, it was more than 18 percent of GDP, representing annual cross-border flows of more than $2.4 trillion,[3] with the aggregate cross-

---

[1] The President's Advisory Panel on Federal Tax Reform (2005).

[2] U.S. Department of Commerce (2007).

[3] U.S. Department of the Treasury (2007).

border ownership of capital valued at roughly $26 trillion.[4] In addition, U.S. multinational corporations are now responsible for more than one-quarter of U.S. output and about 15 percent of U.S. employment.

The internationalization of the world economy has made it imprudent for the United States, or any other country, to enact tax rules that do not take into account what other countries are doing. The U.S. system for taxing businesses should not hinder the ability of U.S. businesses to compete on a global scale. Thus, maintaining the competitiveness of the U.S. economy requires that the United States re-evaluate the current business tax system and consider how it can be designed to ensure that the United States continues to attract and generate the investment and innovation necessary to further advance the living standards of U.S. workers.

This chapter follows up the Treasury Department's July 26th conference. It extends the discussion of business tax reform contained in the Tax Panel's report by focusing on the treatment of business and capital income, and it is shaped by the discussion at the conference on competitiveness. This chapter discusses three bold approaches for business tax reform: (1) a business activity tax (BAT) (a type of consumption tax), while retaining taxes on capital income through the individual income tax, (2) a broad-based, low-rate business income tax, potentially combined with the exemption of active foreign earnings, and (3) a broad-based business tax system with faster write-off of business investment, also potentially combined with the exemption of active foreign earnings. In addition, it provides ideas for other changes that could improve the current business income tax system.

B. BUSINESS TAX REFORM AND THE ECONOMY

Since 1980, the United States has gone from a high corporate tax-rate country to a low-rate country (following the Tax Reform Act of 1986) and, based on some measures, back again to a high-rate country today because other countries recently have reduced their statutory corporate tax rates. Within the Organisation for Economic Co-operation and Development (OECD), the United States now has the second highest statutory corporate tax rate at 39 percent (including state corporate taxes) compared with the average OECD statutory tax rate of 31 percent.

Other countries continue to reduce their corporate tax rates. Germany will reduce its total corporate tax rate from 38 percent to 30 percent in 2008. The

---

[4] International Monetary Fund (2005).

United Kingdom will reduce its corporate tax rate from 30 percent to 28 percent next year. France and Italy have signaled that they may also lower their corporate tax rates. Smaller countries among the OECD also have been particularly aggressive in cutting their corporate tax rates, with Iceland, Ireland, Hungary, Poland, the Slovak Republic, Greece, Korea, and Luxembourg reducing their corporate tax rates significantly in recent years.

Maximizing economic efficiency generally requires that a tax system raise a given amount of revenue with the least possible interference in economic decisions. The

United States' current system for taxing businesses and multinational companies has been developed in a patchwork fashion spanning decades, resulting in a web of tax rules that are unlikely to promote maximum economic efficiency.

The U.S. tax system also disrupts and distorts business and investment decisions, leading to an inefficient level and allocation of capital through the economy. A smaller and poorly allocated stock of capital lowers the productive capacity of the economy and reduces living standards. Importantly, workers share in these economic losses because they have less productive capital with which to work, and thus earn lower wages.

Taxation of Saving and Investment

A key policy question is the appropriate level of tax on the return to saving and investment. Taxes on capital income discourage saving and capital formation. Reduced capital formation provides labor less capital with which to work, lowering labor productivity and, consequently, living standards. Moreover, with the continuing decline in corporate tax rates abroad, the United States may become a relatively less attractive location in which to invest, further reducing U.S. labor productivity and living standards.

The U.S. tax system also taxes investment income very unevenly across sectors, industries, asset types, and financing. Uneven taxation causes investment decisions to be based in part on tax considerations rather than on the fundamental economic merit of investment projects. For example, the United States taxes profits from an equity-financed investment in the corporate sector more heavily than the return earned on other investments. Corporate profits are heavily taxed because they are subject to multiple layers of tax: the corporate income tax, investor-level taxes on capital gains and dividends, and the estate tax.

The multiple taxation of corporate profits distorts a number of economic decisions important to a healthy economy. It distorts corporate financing choices by taxing interest earned on corporate bonds less heavily than corporate profits. As a result, corporations are induced to use more debt than they otherwise would. It distorts corporate distribution policy by taxing dividends more heavily than corporate earnings that are retained and later realized as capital gains (primarily due to the deferral of gains until sale and the opportunity for step-up of stock basis at death). As a result, it confounds market signals of a company's financial health and may have important implications for corporate governance. It also penalizes investment in the corporate form by taxing corporate income more heavily than other capital income. Consequently, it discourages investment in and through corporations in favor of investment in other less heavily taxed business forms (such as partnerships) or in non-business assets (such as owner-occupied housing). The double tax on corporate profits was reduced in 2003 with the enactment of lower tax rates on dividends and capital gains, although this relief, which focused primarily on equity-financed investment, did not completely remove the double tax.

In contrast to corporate profits, the U.S. tax system taxes the returns to many other important investments very lightly, if at all. For example, some business investment is eligible for special tax treatment, and the return earned on investment in residential housing typically is not taxed at all. In some cases, special tax provisions are so generous that they actually subsidize the investment by making the net tax burden negative. These special tax provisions can encourage over-investment in the tax-favored activity. Even where they do not encourage over-investment, they substantially narrow the tax base and drive other tax rates higher, which may distort choices elsewhere in the economy. In addition, special tax provisions add complexity to the tax system and contribute to a substantial business tax compliance burden on the economy, estimated at $40 billion annually for business taxpayers.[5]

Taxation of Flow-through Businesses

The individual income tax also is important to the taxation of businesses. The non-corporate business sector and certain corporations (i.e., flow-through entities such as sole proprietorships, partnerships, and S corporations) are subject to the individual income tax on the business income of the owners or partners. Many of these businesses are small and are an important source of innovation and risk taking in the economy. These businesses and their owners

---

[5] Slemrod (2005).

benefited from the 2001 and 2003 income tax rate reductions. According to estimates by the Treasury Department, roughly 30 percent of all business taxes are paid through the individual income tax on business income earned by the owners of flow-through entities. The importance of flow-through entities has grown substantially over time. This sector has more than doubled its share of all business receipts since the early 1980s, and plays a more important role in the U.S. economy as compared to other member countries of the OECD. Flow-through businesses account for one-third of salaries and wages and claim 27 percent of depreciation deductions. Moreover, flow-though income is concentrated in the top two tax brackets, with this group receiving over 70 percent of flow-through income and paying more than 80 percent of the taxes on this income.

Risk of Standing Still

It is important to consider the effects of leaving the system for taxing U.S. businesses unchanged while other nations reform their systems. In general, inaction would make the United States a less attractive place in which to invest, innovate, and grow. The impact of allowing the U.S. tax system to stagnate and fall behind relative to other countries would be modest at first. The United States would see less benefit from inflows of foreign capital and investment, and U.S. firms would face a higher cost of capital than foreign firms, making it more difficult to compete in foreign markets. In the short run, this would translate into slower growth, less productivity, and less employment.

Over the long run, however, the impact of the United States falling further behind its major trading partners is likely to become more dramatic. Industries that are relatively large producers or users of capital goods would be most affected. American manufacturers, for example, would find themselves especially disadvantaged by a tax code that causes them to face a higher cost of capital than their competitors in other countries. In a world of greater economic integration and increased trade and capital flows, a firm's decision about where to locate and expand its operations would be increasingly influenced by factors such as a country's corporate tax code and overall investment climate.[6]

The current U.S. tax system clearly is not optimal and likely discourages investment in the United States. A more disturbing possibility is that the U.S. tax system may also slow the pace of technological innovation. The pace of innovation is a key determinant of economic growth, and innovation tends to

---

[6] See Altshuler, Grubert, and Newlon (2001).

take place where the investment climate is best. For example, new technologies are often "embedded" in new types of capital – a firm does not benefit from an increase in computer processing speed, for example, unless it purchases a new computer that incorporates the faster chip. Thus, firms do not reap the benefits of technological advances until new capital is brought into production. Similarly, higher investment can spur innovation by raising the demand for new technologies. Given this interplay between innovation and capital accumulation, allowing U.S. corporate taxes to become more burdensome relative to the rest of the world could result in a cumulative effect in which U.S. firms fall increasingly behind those in other nations.

In addition, entrepreneurship would likely be more successful in an environment in which tax burdens are lower. Lower business tax rates are associated with increased business formation. The creation of new business enterprises is important in order to bring new ideas and new products to the market and, therefore, represents another channel by which business taxes can potentially influence innovation.

Reforming the U.S. business tax system would raise capital accumulation and ultimately lead to a higher level of GDP and higher living standards for Americans. Some of this improvement in living standards may result from other economic effects, including the effects of firms relocating their plant and equipment, the additional dynamic effects of bringing new, more effective techniques into production, and potential effects on entrepreneurship. As capital moves more freely across borders, and emerging countries begin to approach U.S. levels of education and training, advantages that the United States currently has will erode. Tax burden differentials may become more important going forward than they have been in the past and, right now, the United States is becoming less competitive in that regard.

C. How Business Taxation in the United States Compares with that of the United States' Major Trading Partners

In an increasingly global economy, the choices that the United States makes for business taxation affect the ability of its businesses to compete with foreign firms subject to different tax regimes. A comparison of the U.S. tax regime with those of the United States' major trading partners may provide important guidance to U.S. business tax reform.

International Comparison of Corporate and Investor-Level Taxes

Statutory Corporate Income Tax Rates

Statutory corporate income tax (CIT) rates are the most common measure of the tax burden imposed on corporations. The first column of table 1.1 shows total statutory CIT rates, incorporating sub-national taxes, where relevant, for OECD countries. The United States has the second highest statutory CIT rate (39 percent) in the OECD after Japan (40 percent). This compares with an average rate of 31 percent for the major industrialized economies.

The evolution of OECD corporate tax rates over the past two decades suggests that CIT rate setting is an interactive process subject to the pressures of international competition. Chart 1.1 shows the U.S. statutory CIT rate compared to the overall OECD rate weighted by GDP since 1982. In the early 1 980s, the United States had a relatively high statutory CIT tax rate of nearly 50 percent (i.e., combined federal and average state CIT rate). The Tax Reform Act of 1986 lowered the U.S. federal CIT rate to 34 percent, and the U.S. combined CIT rate fell to 38 percent, well below the then prevailing OECD CIT rates. OECD rates trended steadily down over the ensuing decade, while the top U.S. federal CIT rate was increased to 35 percent in 1993. The average and median OECD statutory CIT rates fell below the U.S. CIT rate in the 1990s and have continued to decline. Now, the United States is once again a high corporate tax rate country. The decline in OECD corporate tax rates appears likely to continue. In 2008, Germany will reduce its CIT rate from 38 percent to 30 percent, and the United Kingdom will reduce its CIT rate from 30 percent to 28 percent, financed by base broadening. Italy's government has proposed lowering its corporate tax rate from 33 percent to 27.5 percent in 2008, and cutting corporate taxes is also part of the current French government's policy platform.[7]

---

[7] BNA, Daily Tax Report (2007), Market News International (2007).

Table 1.1. Statutory Corporate Income Tax Rates, Depreciation Allowances and Effective Marginal Tax Rates for Selected OECD Countries, 2005

Country	Statutory Corporate Income Tax Rate	Present Discounted Value of Depreciation Allowance Equipment (Equity)	Effective Marginal Tax Rate* Equipment (Equity)	Effective Marginal Tax Rate* Equipment (Debt)
Percent				
Australia	30	66	24	-23
Austria	25	66	20	-18
Belgium	34	75	22	-35
Canada	36	73	25	-37
Finland	26	73	17	-23
France	34	77	20	-36
United Kingdom	30	73	20	-28
Germany	38	71	29	-37
Greece	32	87	12	-40
Ireland	13	66	10	-8
Italy	37	82	19	-48
Japan	40	73	28	-40
Netherlands	32	73	21	-29
Norway	28	67	22	-21
Portugal	28	79	15	-29
Spain	35	78	21	-38
Sweden	28	78	16	-29
Switzerland	34	78	20	-36
United States	39	79	24	-46
Average (Unweighted)	31	75	20	-32
G-7 Average (Unweighted)	36	76	24	-39

* Effective Marginal Tax Rates (EMTRs) are discussed in the following section. Source: Institute for Fiscal Studies, Corporate Tax Database, www.ifs.org.uk.

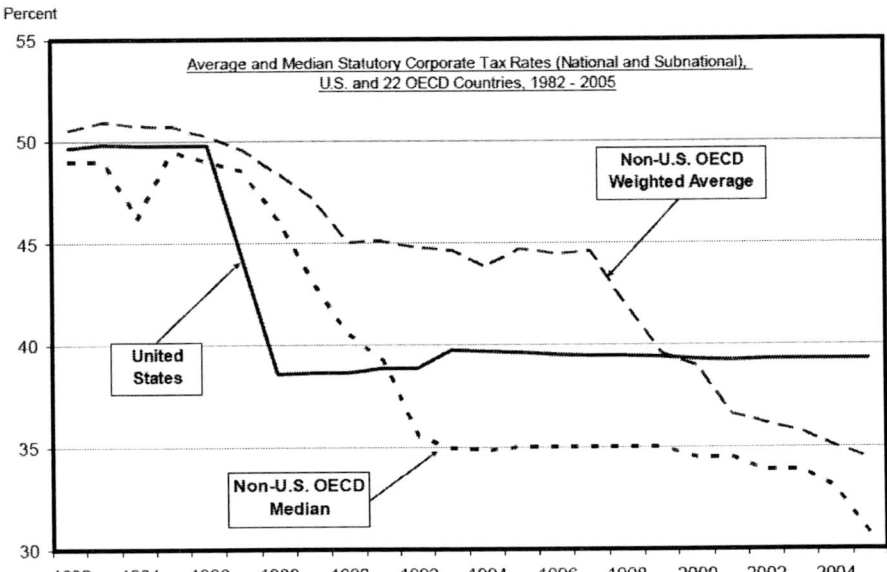

Source: Institute for Fiscal Studies (www.ifs.org) and the Organisation for Economic Co-operation and Development (www.oecd.org).

Chart 1.1. The U.S. Corporate Tax Rate Currently Exceeds the Average OECD Corporate Tax Rate.

Several factors contribute to the increased competition in corporate tax rates. The rapid increase in international capital mobility over the past two decades has made corporate investment more sensitive to relative CIT rates. Capital market integration has been particularly pronounced within the European Union, whose members' ongoing CIT reductions are, to some degree, reacting to the low CIT rates in Eastern Europe. Increasingly sophisticated tax planning methods may also be contributing to increased tax competition among OECD countries.

Effective Marginal Tax Rates (EMTRs)

Statutory corporate tax rates provide an incomplete picture of the corporate tax burden because they reflect neither the corporate tax base nor investor-level taxes. Depreciation allowances – the rate at which capital investment costs may be deducted from taxable income over time – are a key determinant of the corporate tax base and an important factor distinguishing the statutory CIT rate from the effective marginal CIT rate (EMTRs). The EMTR combines corporate tax rates, depreciation allowances, and other features of the tax system into a single measure of the share of an investment's economic income needed to cover taxes over its lifetime. This measure of the "tax wedge" between the before-tax and after-tax return on an investment is measured relative to the before-tax return.

The EMTR varies depending on the source of finance – debt or equity – because interest is generally deductible, but dividends are not. The required rate of return for debt-financed investment, therefore, is lower than the required return for equity-financed investment in proportion to the CIT rate. This lower discount rate also increases the present discounted value (PDV) of depreciation allowances for debt-financed investment. In fact, due to interest deductibility and accelerated depreciation, the corporate EMTR on debt-financed investment is negative for all OECD countries, implying a tax subsidy for debt-financed investment. (However, incorporation of individual-level taxes on interest income generally restores taxation of debt-financed investment to a positive rate.) Thus, in addition to affecting the allocation of capital across borders, the corporate tax also affects financing decisions, favoring the use of debt finance instead of equity finance.

Column 2 of table 1.1 shows the importance of depreciation allowances for explaining differences in corporate tax bases (and EMTRs) for OECD countries. A PDV of one is equivalent to immediate write-off (expensing) of investment, while a PDV of zero means that investment is non-depreciable. If the rate of tax depreciation equals the rate of economic depreciation (and there is zero inflation), then the EMTR for equity- financed investment equals the statutory CIT rate (and the EMTR on debt-financed investment equals zero). Most OECD countries offer accelerated depreciation for equipment investment, such that their equity EMTRs are lower than their statutory tax rates. In contrast to its high statutory CIT rate, the United States has relatively generous depreciation allowances for equipment, with a PDV of 79 percent. In the OECD, only Greece and Italy have more generous depreciation allowances.

The trend in OECD depreciation allowances over the past two decades has been toward slower depreciation, as countries have at least partially offset CIT rate cuts with corporate base broadening. According to the Institute for Fiscal Studies, the average PDV of OECD depreciation allowances fell from 82 percent in 1980 to 75 percent in 2005. Depreciation allowances among the G-7 also declined during the same period, but remained generally higher, falling from 85 percent to 76 percent.[8]

---

[8] Institute for Fiscal Studies, Corporate Tax Database, www.ifs.org.uk

The corporate EMTRs for equity-financed and debt-financed equipment investment, respectively, for the OECD countries are shown in Columns 3 and 4 of table 1.1. The U.S. EMTR for equity-financed equipment investment, 24 percent, is above the OECD average of 20 percent, but equal to the G-7 average. The U.S. EMTR for debt- financed investment in equipment, -46 percent, is below average for both the G-7 (-39 percent) and the OECD (-32 percent). These figures illustrate the divergent influence of statutory CIT rates on equity and debt EMTRs. A higher CIT rate produces a higher equity EMTR but a lower debt EMTR because the value of the interest deduction increases with the corporate tax rate. The above-average U.S. statutory CIT rate thus contributes to a below-average debt EMTR. Indeed, the United States has the greatest disparity between debt and equity EMTRs in the OECD, possibly resulting in a more pronounced tax bias of financing decisions in the United States than in other OECD countries.

To gauge the net effect of statutory CIT rates and the size of the corporate tax base, empirical measures of the average corporate tax rate are sometimes considered, such as the ratio of corporate income tax revenues to gross domestic product (GDP).

Over the period of 2000 through 2005, the average ratio of corporate income tax revenues to GDP for the OECD was 3.5 percent; for the United States, the average ratio was 2.2 percent. Thus, the high U.S. corporate tax rate does not result in higher corporate tax revenue relative to GDP due to the narrowness of the U.S. corporate tax base. The narrow corporate tax base results not only from accelerated depreciation allowances, but also from special tax provisions for particular business sectors (such as domestic production activities) as well as debt finance and tax planning.

Emerging Market Countries

Because U.S. corporations are increasingly investing in and competing with corporations in emerging markets, comparison of the U.S. corporate tax regime with those of major emerging market countries is also important. Table 1.2 shows statutory CIT rates, depreciation allowances, and corporate effective marginal tax rates for three large, emerging market U.S. trading partners – China, India, and Mexico. Their domestic statutory CIT rates are fairly close to the OECD average of 31 percent. However, both China and India have levied corporate tax on domestic and foreign investors at different rates. In China, while the total statutory CIT rate on domestic firms was 31 percent (equal to the OECD average), special low rates of 15 percent to 24 percent were accorded foreign corporations investing in particular sectors and geographic regions. Although

China has recently passed legislation that will unify its domestic and foreign corporate tax rate at 25 percent – substantially below the OECD average – it will continue to offer special tax relief for investment in particular sectors and regions. India, conversely, taxes foreign investors more heavily than domestic firms. The statutory CIT rate faced by foreign corporations is more than 10 percentage points higher than the 34-percent rate levied on domestic firms. Mexico's statutory tax rate, 32 percent, is slightly above the OECD average.

Table 1.2. U.S. vs. Emerging Market Country Tax Rates, 2006

Country	Statutory Corporate Tax Rate		PDV of Depreciation Allowance -Equipment (Equity)	EMTR Equipment (Equity)
	Domestic	Foreign	Domestic	Domestic
Percent				
China*	31	15-24	48	34
India	34	45	51	36
Mexico	32	32	53	33
United States	39	39	79	24

* Foreign investment in Chinese special enterprise zones is subject to a 15 percent or 24 percent CIT rate. China has passed legislation to unify its domestic and foreign corporate tax rates at 25 percent.
Source: International Bureau of Fiscal Documentation (2007b).

Depreciation allowances in these three emerging market countries, which have an average PDV of 51 percent, are markedly less favorable than the OECD average of 75 percent. Despite having domestic statutory CIT rates roughly equal to the OECD average, these three countries' broad corporate tax bases result in equity EMTRs that, with an average rate of 34 percent, are well above the OECD average of 20 percent.

Individual-Level Taxation of Corporate Income

Firm-level taxation provides an incomplete picture of the tax burden on corporate investment because corporate profits distributed in the form of interest, dividends, and capital gains are often subject to a second level of tax at the investor level. Because interest is deductible by the corporation, debt-financed investment is subject to only a single layer of tax at the investor level. However, dividends and retained earnings (which produce capital gains) may not be deducted by the corporation, so that equity-financed investment is frequently subject to "double taxation" – it is taxed first under the corporate income tax and then again under the individual income tax when distributed to investors as dividends or retained by the corporation and realized by investors as capital gains.[9]

The importance of investor-level taxes for affecting investment decisions depends on the tax rate faced by the marginal investor. If the marginal corporate investor is tax- exempt (such as a pension fund), then the corporate-level EMTR alone describes marginal investment incentives in the corporate sector. However, if the marginal investor is subject to taxes on corporate interest, dividends, and capital gains, then that layer also needs to be taken into account in calculating the EMTR on corporate investment. Typically, it is assumed that the marginal investor is a weighted average of business taxpayers that are tax-exempt and taxpayers who are subject to investor-level taxes.

Most countries offer some type of integration scheme to alleviate double taxation, which usually takes the form of either: (1) reduced tax rates on (long-term) capital gains and dividends, (2) a tax imputation system, which gives the investor credit for part or all of the tax paid at the corporate level, or (3) a dividend exclusion combined with basis adjustments for corporate income that is retained by the firm. Another increasingly popular method of capital income taxation, sometimes referred to as the "Scandinavian system," is to tax interest, dividends, and capital gains at a single rate well below the top marginal rate on earned income.

OECD countries offering partial or full imputation of dividend taxes include the United Kingdom, Canada, and Mexico. The United States, Japan, and India offer reduced tax rates on long-term capital gains (which the United States currently also applies to dividends), while Germany and France offer a 50-percent exclusion of dividend income. Countries that have adopted Scandinavian systems include Italy and China.[10]

Table 1.3 shows the top statutory tax rates levied on residents' receipts of interest, dividends, and capital gains for the G-7 countries. The United States has an above- average tax rate on interest, a below-average tax rate on dividends, and an average tax rate on long-term capital gains. Table 1.4 shows the integrated EMTRs for the G-7 countries calculated for a taxable domestic investor in the top marginal income tax bracket. The United States has an above-average EMTR for equipment investment financed with debt or retained earnings, and a roughly average EMTR for investment financed with new share issues.

---

[9] The return to these investments may be taxed again under the estate tax.
[10] OECD, Tax Database, www.oecd.org

Table 1.3. Top Investor-Level Capital Income Tax Rates for the G-7, 2006

Country	Interest Tax Rate	Dividend Tax Rate	Capital Gains Tax Rate
Percent			
Canada	46.4	30.0	23.2
France	27.0	23.0	26.0
Germany	47.5	23.7	23.7
Italy	12.5	12.5	20.0
Japan	16.3	30.0	10.0
United Kingdom	40.0	25.1	10.0
United States	37.9	18.8	18.8
Unweighted average	32.5	23.3	18.8

Note: Where applicable, data include sub-national tax rates, dividend tax rates incorporate integration allowances, and tax rates are for long-term, large-scale investment.
Source: International Bureau of Fiscal Documentation (2007a).

Worldwide vs. Territorial Systems

Another respect in which the U.S. corporate tax system differs from that of the majority of the United States' trading partners is in its taxation of corporations' worldwide earnings. U.S. corporations pay tax on the active earnings of their foreign subsidiaries when those earnings are paid out as dividends to their parent corporations (although credit is given for taxes paid on those earnings to foreign governments). The major alternative to a worldwide system is a territorial system in which the home country exempts all or a portion of foreign earnings from home-country taxation.

Although a predominantly worldwide approach to the taxation of cross-border income was once prevalent, table 1.5 shows that it is now used by roughly less than one-half of OECD countries. Instead, many of these countries now use predominantly territorial tax systems. To protect the integrity of investor-level taxes under the individual income tax system, however, countries with predominantly territorial systems typically do not exempt certain foreign earnings of foreign subsidiaries, including earnings generated from holding mobile financial assets, or certain payments that are deductible in the jurisdiction from which the payment is made, such as foreign source royalty payments.

Table 1.4. Integrated Effective Marginal Tax Rates for G-7 Countries, 2006

Country	Debt	New Shares*	Retained Earnings**
		Percent	
Canada	51.8	63.4	51.8
France	12.6	49.9	43.7
Germany	56.8	64.0	58.7
Italy	-29.7	29.0	28.3
Japan	-49.0	49.9	25.3
United Kingdom	46.1	55.8	38.8
United States	31.0	51.8	46.1
Unweighted average	17.1	52.0	41.8

*The applicable tax rate for new share issues is the tax on dividends.
**The applicable tax rate for retained earnings is the tax on long-term capital gains.
The effective marginal tax rates on retained earnings assume 10 years of deferral.
Source: International Bureau of Fiscal Documentation (2007a).

Consumption Taxes

Another respect in which the U.S. tax system differs markedly from that of the United States' major trading partners is the reliance on consumption taxes. Table 1.6 shows OECD countries' usage of taxes on goods and services[11] and taxes on general consumption.[12] It also shows the standard value-added tax (VAT) rate in OECD countries. The United States relies less heavily on taxes on goods and services than all other OECD countries, measured both as a percentage of GDP and as a share of total taxation.[13] As a percentage of GDP, taxes on goods and services in 2005 were 4.8 percent in the United States compared with the OECD average of 11.4 percent. As a percentage of total taxation, taxes on goods and services were 17.4 percent in the United States compared with the OECD average of 31.9 percent. Japan was the only other OECD country that was similar to the

---

[11] Taxes on goods and services include all taxes and duties levied on the production, extraction, sale, transfer, leasing or delivery of goods, and the rendering of services, and certain other taxes.

[12] General consumption taxes include value-added taxes, sales taxes and multi-stage cumulative taxes.

[13] The tax levied in the United States on goods and services is imposed by most states in the form of retail sales taxes.

United States using those measures – taxes on goods and services were 5.3 percent of GDP and 19.4 percent of total taxation.

Table 1.5. Territorial vs. Worldwide Treatment of Foreign Dividend Income by Country, 2005

Territorial (Exemption)	Worldwide (Foreign Tax Credit)
Australia*	Czech Republic
Austria	Ireland
Belgium	Japan
Canada*	Korea
Denmark	Mexico
Finland	New Zealand
France**	Poland
Germany	United Kingdom
Greece*	United States
Hungary	
Italy**	
Luxembourg	
Netherlands	
Norway	
Portugal*	
Slovak Republic	
Spain	
Sweden	
Switzerland	
Turkey	

*Exemption by treaty agreement. **Exemption of 95 percent.
Source: President's Advisory Panel on Federal Tax Reform (2005).

The United States also relies less heavily on general consumption taxes (such as VATs and general sales taxes) than all other OECD countries. As a percentage of GDP, general consumption taxes in 2005 were 2.2 percent in the United States compared with the OECD average of 6.9 percent. As a percentage of total taxation, general consumption taxes were 8.0 percent in the United States compared with the OECD average of 18.9 percent. Japan was the only other OECD country that was similar to the United States using those measures – general consumption taxes were 2.6 percent of GDP and 9.5 percent of total taxation. Finally, the United States is the only OECD country without a VAT, although most states impose retail sales taxes.

Table 1.6. Consumption Taxes among OECD Countries

Country	Taxes on Goods and Services*		Taxes on General Consumption*		Value-Added Taxation**
	Percentage of GDP	Percentage of Total Taxation	Percentage of GDP	Percentage of Total Taxation	Standard VAT Rate
Percent					
Australia	8.6	27.8	4.1	13.4	10.0
Austria	12.0	28.4	7.9	18.9	20.0
Belgium	11.5	25.3	7.3	16.1	21.0
Canada	8.5	25.4	5.0	15.0	7.0
Czech Republic	11.8	31.3	7.2	19.2	19.0
Denmark	16.2	32.2	10.0	19.9	25.0
Finland	13.8	31.3	8.7	19.8	22.0
France	11.2	25.3	7.8	17.1	19.6
Germany	10.1	29.0	6.3	18.0	16.0
Greece	9.4	34.6	6.0	22.2	19.0
Hungary	14.8	39.7	10.5	28.1	20.0
Iceland	16.7	40.4	11.5	27.7	24.5
Ireland	11.6	37.8	7.7	25.1	21.0
Italy	10.8	26.4	6.0	14.6	20.0
Japan	5.3	19.4	2.6	9.5	5.0
Korea	8.8	34.3	4.5	17.5	10.0
Luxembourg	11.1	28.8	6.2	16.1	15.0
Mexico	11.3	56.7	3.8	19.1	15.0
Netherlands	12.4	31.7	7.6	19.5	19.0
New Zealand	12.1	32.1	9.0	23.8	12.5
Norway	12.2	27.9	7.9	18.1	25.0
Poland	12.6	36.7	7.7	22.5	22.0
Portugal	13.6	39.3	8.3	23.8	21.0
Slovak Republic	12.5	39.7	7.9	25.1	19.0
Spain	10.0	28.0	6.2	17.5	16.0
Sweden	13.2	26.1	9.4	18.5	25.0
Switzerland	7.0	23.6	4.0	13.4	7.6
Turkey	15.9	49.3	7.1	21.8	18.0
United Kingdom	11.1	30.3	6.8	18.6	17.5

	Taxes on Goods and Services*		Taxes on General Consumption*		Value-Added Taxation**
Country	Percentage of GDP	Percentage of Total Taxation	Percentage of GDP	Percentage of Total Taxation	Standard VAT Rate
Percent					
United States	4.8	17.4	2.2	8.0	0.0
Unweighted Average	11.4	31.9	6.9	18.9	17.1

*Figures are for 2005. **Figures are for 2006.
Source: OECD, *Revenue Statistics* (2007) and OECD Tax Database, www.oecd.org.

D. SUMMARY

The U.S business tax system has not kept pace with changes in the global economy. The tax reforms enacted by the United States in the 1 980s were followed by reforms in other countries. The U.S. statutory corporate income tax rate is now the second highest among the OECD countries, and the U.S. corporate effective marginal tax rate is roughly average, discouraging both foreign direct investment and labor productivity.

The U.S. system for taxing businesses differs from those in other OECD countries in other important respects. The United States taxes corporations on their worldwide earnings, a once prevalent approach now used by less than one-half of OECD countries. Instead, many countries use predominantly territorial systems that exempt all or a portion of foreign active earnings from home-country taxation. In addition, the United States relies less heavily on consumption taxes than other OECD countries and is the only OECD country that does not have a VAT.

The current U.S. system for taxing businesses clearly is not optimal. It includes ad hoc policies and special tax provisions that narrow the tax base and create distortions that divert capital from its most efficient use. This lowers the productive capacity of the economy.

The U.S. business tax system needs to be designed to help U.S. companies and workers compete by taking into account the increasingly integrated global economy. With a view to future competitiveness, U.S. tax policy must respond to and anticipate changes in the global marketplace. The U.S. system for taxing businesses needs to be reevaluated to consider how it can be improved to attract and generate the investment and innovation necessary to advance the living standards of all Americans.

The remainder of this chapter discusses approaches that could be considered for reforming the taxation of business income. Chapter II examines an approach that would replace business income taxes with a BAT (a type of consumption tax), while retaining taxes on capital income through the individual income tax. Chapter III explores an approach that would broaden the income tax base and use the revenues either to lower business income tax rates or permit more rapid write-off of business investment, potentially combined with the exemption of foreign active earnings. Chapter IV discusses specific areas of business income taxation that could be reformed separately or in the context of a broad-based reform.

REFERENCES

Altshuler, Rosanne H., Harry Grubert, and T. Scott Newlon. 2001. "Has U.S. Investment Abroad Become More Sensitive to Tax Rates? In *International Taxation and Multinational Activity 2001*, ed. J. Hines, 9-32. Chicago: University of Chicago Press.

BNA Daily Tax Report. 2007. "Italian Tax Reform Embedded in Country's Budget Law for 2008," October 24, 2007. www.bna.com

Hodge, Scott A. and Chris Atkins. 2007. "U.S. Still Lagging Behind OECD Corporate Tax Trends." *Tax Foundation Fiscal Fact No. 96.*

Institute for Fiscal Studies, Corporate Tax Database, www.ifs.org.uk

International Bureau of Fiscal Documentation. 2007a. *European Tax Handbook.* Amsterdam: International Bureau of Fiscal Documentation.

International Bureau of Fiscal Documentation. 2007b. *Taxes and Investment in Asia and the Pacific.* Amsterdam: International Bureau of Fiscal Documentation.

International Monetary Fund. 2005. *International Monetary Fund Coordinated Portfolio Investment Survey.*

Kahn, Gabriel and Luca di Leo. 2007. "Italy's Budget Targets Boosting Fiscal Order," *Wall Street Journal* October 1, 2007.

KPMG. 2007. *KPMG's Corporate Tax Rate Survey, 2007.*

Market News International. 2007. "France Elections: Economic Platforms of Sarkozy and Royal," April 23, 2007. www.marketnews.com

Organisation for Economic Co-operation and Development, Tax Database, www.oecd.org

Organisation for Economic Co-operation and Development. 2007. *Revenue Statistics 2007*. Paris: Organisation for Economic Co-operation and Development.

Organisation for Economic Co-operation and Development. Forthcoming. *Tax Effects on Foreign Direct Investment: Recent Evidence and Policy Analysis*. Paris: Organisation for Economic Co-operation and Development.

President's Advisory Panel on Federal Tax Reform. 2005. *Simple, Fair and Pro-Growth: Proposals to Fix America's Tax System*. Washington, DC: U.S. Government Printing Office.

Slemrod, Joel. 2005. "The Costs of Tax Complexity," Presentation to the President's Advisory Panel on Federal Tax Reform, March 3, 2005.

The Economic Times. 2007. "FM Hints at Tax Cuts, Yields to Area-Wise Incentives." August 1, 2007.

U.S. Department of Commerce. 2007. Bureau of Economic Analysis news release, November 2007. http://www.bea.gov/newsreleases/national/ gdp/2007/pdf/ gdp307p.pdf

U.S. Department of the Treasury, Office of Tax Analysis. 2006. *A Dynamic Analysis of Permanent Extension of the President's Tax Relief*. Washington, DC: U.S. Department of the Treasury, July 25, 2006. http://www.treas.gov/press/releases/reports/treasurydynamicanalysisreporj july252 006 .pdf

U.S. Department of the Treasury. 2007. *Report on Foreign Portfolio Holdings of U.S. Securities*. Washington, DC: U.S. Department of the Treasury, June 2007. http://www.treasury.gov/tic/shl2006r.pdf

U.S. Department of the Treasury. 2007. *Treasury Conference on Business Taxation and Global Competitiveness: Background Paper*. Washington, DC: U.S. Department of the Treasury, July 23, 2007. http://www.treas.gov/press/ releases/reports/07230%20r.pdf

Chapter 2

REPLACING BUSINESS INCOME TAXES WITH A BUSINESS ACTIVITIES TAX

A. INTRODUCTION

This chapter examines replacing present U.S. business income taxes with a broad- based Business Activities Tax (BAT), which is a type of consumption tax. Assuming a very broad base, a BAT imposed at a rate of roughly 5 percent to 6 percent would replace the revenue from current U.S. business income taxes.

Under this approach the corporate income tax as well as the existing individual income taxes collected from pass-through entities (partnerships, sole proprietorships, and S corporations) would be replaced with a BAT. While business income taxes would be repealed and replaced by a BAT, the individual income tax that includes investor-level taxes on dividends and capital gains would be retained, and the tax treatment of interest received by individuals would be conformed to that for dividends and capital gains (i.e., taxed at the lower rates currently available for dividends and capital gains).

For two reasons, this approach is estimated to improve economic performance, ultimately increasing the size of the economy by roughly 2.0 percent to 2.5 percent. First, because a BAT does not tax the normal return to saving or investment,[14] it is likely to stimulate additional saving and investment. Greater investment means businesses would have more capital, which increases workers' productivity, and ultimately improves living standards. Second, it

---

[14] See Box 2.2 below for a description of the normal return to saving or investment.

would likely reduce a variety of tax distortions that arise under the current tax system due to the uneven treatment of investment and other economic activity.[15]

Because this approach entails repeal of the corporate income tax but retains the individual income tax, it could create incentives for individuals to accumulate passive investment income in the corporate form to defer or avoid paying individual investor- level taxes on such income. It also could create incentives for business owners to minimize payments for their own labor services, which would not be deductible, to avoid income and payroll taxes. These issues could be addressed through special rules, which could create additional complexity. Other distortions may arise because a BAT base is unlikely to cover all consumer goods and services. For example, taxing consumer financial services under a BAT is difficult in practice and small businesses are often exempt from consumption taxes in other countries for administrative reasons.

The remainder of this chapter describes a BAT and discusses the economic effects of this approach in more detail. It also describes the main features of the similar value- added taxes (VATs) typically imposed in other countries.

Replacing business income taxes with a BAT would be a bold reform. Indeed, it is a reform that has not been attempted in other countries. Nevertheless, it is possible to overemphasize the novelty of a BAT for the United States. Although perhaps not universally understood, the actual U.S. tax system is not a pure income tax, but a hybrid combination of an income tax and a consumption tax.[16] The U.S. tax system already has important features that move in the direction of a BAT. For example, accelerated depreciation is a step toward the immediate deduction of the cost of an investment that would be allowed by a BAT. Further, certain investment costs, such as investments undertaken by certain small businesses and the costs of producing certain intangibles, are currently allowed an immediate deduction, the same treatment as under a BAT. Thus, while the BAT approach outlined in this chapter is a consumption tax, it is worth noting that the U.S. tax system currently has some features that are similar.

---

[15] The estimate of the improvement in economic performance includes the effect of reducing distortions among investments in different sectors (such as the distortion between investment in the corporate sector and investment in owner-occupied housing), but does not include the effect of reducing distortions in the treatment of investment in different assets within the business sector (such as distortion in the treatment of investment in equipment and investment in buildings).

[16] Auerbach (1996).

B. Description of a BAT

A BAT is a tax on goods and services sold to consumers. Under a BAT, the tax base for each firm is the gross receipts from the sales of goods and services minus purchases of goods and services (including purchases of capital goods) from other businesses. Wages and other forms of employee compensation (such as fringe benefits) are not deductible and, therefore, the effective tax rate on labor could be increased, as discussed below. Under a BAT, financial flows, such as interest and dividends (whether received or paid), would not enter into the tax base. For the economy as a whole, the tax base of a BAT is the sales of real goods and services to consumers, because sales from one business to another have been deducted from the tax base.

A BAT is similar to the VATs imposed in many countries around the world. These VATs, however, generally use a credit-invoice method. In contrast, a BAT uses a deduction or subtraction method for calculating the tax.[17] In a credit-invoice method, a business is taxed on all receipts but receives a credit for the amount of tax paid by the seller on the business' purchases.[18] A BAT is also similar to a broad-based retail sales tax.[19]

Calculation of a BAT

To understand how a BAT works, consider the illustration below (table 2.1) of how bread produced by a farmer, miller, and baker would be taxed under a BAT with a 10-percent tax rate. In this example, the farmer grows wheat and sells it to the miller, who makes flour for sale to the baker. In turn, the baker uses the flour to make bread, which is then sold to consumers.

---

[17] Japan, however, operates a VAT with many subtraction method features. The Japanese VAT uses an annual accounting period, and taxpayers subject to the Japanese VAT derive the amount of their applicable credit for the VAT paid based on their total purchases from domestic entities, rather than based on the VAT paid as shown in a credit-invoice method. See Schenk (1995) and Japanese Ministry of Finance, Tax Bureau (2005). A BAT would have similarities to the current U.S. business tax system by having an annual tax period and a tax return submitted by businesses to the taxing authority.

[18] In some countries, the credit-invoice VAT is referred to as a Goods and Services Tax (GST).

[19] Sales taxes levied by state and local governments differ considerably from the ideal retail sales tax for many reasons, including the fact that some apply to many business-to-business sales that would not be taxed under an ideal retail sales tax or involve substantially narrow tax bases that exempt certain sales.

Table 2.1. Calculation of a BAT

Economic Activity	Farmer	Miller	Baker	Total
Sales	$300	$700	$1,000	
Purchases	$0	$300	$700	
Value added (lines 1-2)	$300	$400	$300	$1,000
BAT (10% of line 3)	$30	$40	$30	$100

Source: Department of the Treasury, Office of Tax Analysis.

A BAT is calculated by subtracting purchases from sales at each stage of the production and distribution process. The baker, for example, applies a 10-percent tax rate to the $300 difference between total bread sales and purchase of grain and owes $30 of BAT. The farmer and the miller calculate tax in the same way and the total BAT paid is $100. This is the same amount of total tax that would be paid under a 10-percent retail sales tax. The only difference is that the 10-percent retail sales tax would be levied only on the final $1,000 sale to consumers.

The BAT Base

In principle, a BAT would tax a broad range of consumption goods and services. Most existing VATs, however, do not tax all consumption.[20] Some goods are excluded for administrative reasons. Other goods are excluded, or taxed at preferentially low rates, in order to pursue policy or social objectives. Nevertheless, keeping the base of a BAT as broad as possible minimizes the distortions caused by the tax.

Total consumption is the broadest conceivable BAT base. However, taxing total consumption would be impractical, if not impossible, for several reasons. First, some goods and services could be difficult to value, such as consumer financial services and government-provided goods and services.[21] Second, other goods and services, while perhaps easy to value, would raise difficult enforcement

---

[20] See chapter III in Congressional Budget Office (1992).

[21] The annual consumption flows from the existing stock of owner-occupied housing and other consumer durables (e.g., automobiles) also would be difficult to value under a BAT. New housing and consumer durables could be taxed on a pre-payment basis. Tax would be imposed on the purchase price, which is equivalent in present value to a tax on the annual consumption flow. For a detailed explanation, see Bradford (1986).

problems. For example, underreporting of sales by small businesses or casual service providers would be a problem under a BAT, as it is under our current tax system. Third, the taxation of some goods and services may raise measurement and bookkeeping challenges (e.g., spending that provides employees compensation that is nondeductible must be identified and separated from other business spending such as business meals). Of course, many of these issues represent significant challenges under our current tax system.

Some goods may be viewed as especially desirable because their consumption benefits society as a whole. Because they provide benefits to others, there may be a policy reason to reduce or eliminate the rate of tax on "merit goods," such as education, health care, welfare services, cultural activities, and religious and charitable activities. Other goods, such as necessities, may be taxed at a low rate in order to reduce the tax burden on the poor. These might include medical care, food, electricity, heating oil and gas, and clothing. A lower rate for necessities is generally viewed as an inefficient way to address perceived regressivity, however, because the wealthy typically consume more than the poor, including with respect to most "necessities." Moreover, such special treatment would require a higher BAT rate for other consumption.

C. ECONOMIC EFFECTS OF A BROAD-BASED BAT

Replacing the present system of business taxes with a broad-based BAT would likely improve economic performance by eliminating features of the present income tax that create economic distortions such as the tax penalty on saving and investment and the uneven taxation of economic activity. The Treasury Department estimates that this approach would ultimately increase the size of the economy by roughly 2.0 percent to 2.5 percent.

Economic Gains from Replacing Business Taxes with a Broad-Based BAT

The economic gains have two primary sources. First, a BAT lowers the tax on the return to saving and investment. (Box 2.1 discusses the effect of a consumption tax on saving and investment.) Replacement of the existing tax on business income with a BAT would lower the effective marginal tax rate on investment from its current level of 17 percent to 8 percent overall, and from 25 percent to 15 percent in the business sector.[22] The lower tax on saving and investment, which is likely to be quantitatively more important for producing economic gains than the more even taxation of economic activity, would increase capital formation, enhance labor productivity, and ultimately, increase living standards.

> **Box 2.1. The Incentive to Save and Invest Under a Consumption Tax**[23]
>
> The key difference between an income tax and a consumption tax is that an income tax discourages savings while a consumption tax does not. Because a consumption tax imposes an equal tax on present and future consumption, it does not discourage saving for future consumption. In contrast, an income tax taxes the return to saving, thereby taxing consumption in the future more heavily than consumption today.
>
> An income tax discourages saving for the future by reducing the after-tax rate of return received by the investor below the pre-tax rate of return produced by the investment.
>
> - An important feature that distinguishes an income tax from a consumption tax lies in how each treats the cost recovery of capital goods (i.e., the tax treatment of investment). Under an income tax, the cost of capital goods is deducted over time through depreciation allowances as the capital goods wear out, which results in the investor's after-tax return falling below the pre-tax return. Under a consumption tax, the cost of capital goods is deducted fully in the year of purchase (i.e., capital is "expensed"), which results in the investor's after-tax return exactly equaling the pre-tax return. This occurs because, under a consumption tax, the value of the expensing deduction exactly offsets the tax on the return to the investment (in present value) for the marginal, or break-even, investment.[24]

---

[22] The effective marginal tax rate combines corporate tax rates, depreciation allowances, and other features of the tax system into a single measure of the share of an investment's economic income needed to cover taxes over its lifetime. This measure of the "tax wedge" between the before-tax and after-tax returns on an investment is measured relative to the before-tax return.

[23] For a detailed discussion, see Slemrod and Bakija (1996).

[24] The full deduction in the year of purchase will offset (in present value) what economists call the expected normal return. Supra-normal returns would continue to be taxed under this type of consumption tax.

These points are illustrated in the following simple example of a business' investment decision under a 20-percent income tax and a 20-percent consumption tax (table 2.2). Consider a business that has earned $1,000 in profit. The business owner must decide whether to invest in a machine that will produce output next year that sells for 10 percent more than the machine's cost, after which the machine is totally worn out. If the business owner does not invest, he will pay $200 in tax on the $1,000 profit and will have $800 to spend on consumption — the same result under both the income tax and the consumption tax.

For each tax, we now enquire: How much consumption can the owner obtain in the second year if he foregoes this $800 of first-year consumption and instead invests? Under the income tax, if the business owner invests in the machine, he will still pay $200 in tax in the first year and can buy an $800 machine. In the next year, given the 10- percent pre-tax rate of return, the machine produces $880 of output, which is taxable. Because the business owner can deduct the full $800 cost of the machine as depreciation in the second year, his taxable income is $80. The tax on the income is $16, and he is left with $864 in cash to consume. The owner gives up $800 consumption in the first year to obtain $864 consumption in the second year. Thus, after taxes he earns a rate of return of 8 percent (($864-$800)/$800), which is less than the 10-percent pre-tax rate of return that the investment produces.

Under a consumption tax, the business owner who invests in the machine could deduct the full $1,000 cost of a machine when it is purchased. This means that the business owner can invest $1,000 in the first year. Compared to consuming the proceeds, investing gives him a first year tax savings of $200, which he invests in the machine. Given a 10-percent pre-tax rate of return, the $1,000 investment in the machine would be worth $1,100 in the next year. All of the $1,100 would be taxable, and there would be no deduction, so that the business owner would be left with $880 after taxes. This $880 leaves him with a 10-percent after-tax rate of return on his investment because the after- tax cost of the $880 in year 2 is the $800 of consumption he gave up in year 1. Under the consumption tax the after-tax rate of return and the pre-tax rate of return are exactly equal. Stated somewhat differently, the time value of money on the $200 in tax savings generated by the investment (i.e., $20 given the 10-percent rate of return) just offsets the tax on the investment's return that is paid in the second year ($20), which eliminates the net tax liability on the rate of return. In present value terms, consumption tax liability is the same regardless of when the business owner consumes.

Table 2.2. Comparison of Taxes on Investment under an Income Tax and a Consumption Tax

	Income Tax	Consumption Tax
Year 1 pre-tax income	$1,000	$1,000
If income is consumed in year 1		
Pre-tax income (= pre-tax consumption)	$1,000	$1,000
Income tax (20%)	$200	na
Consumption tax (20%)	na	$200
After-tax consumption (pre-tax income minus tax)	$800	$800
If income is invested in year 1		
Pre-tax income	$1,000	$1,000
Less deduction for investment cost	$0	$1,000
Income tax (20%)	$200	na
Consumption tax (20% on pre-tax income minus investment)	na	$0
Investment (pre-tax income minus tax)	$800	$1,000
Memo: Taxpayer's cost for the investment (consumption given up)	$800	$800
Potential consumption in year 2		
Pre-tax cash-flow (i = 10%)	$880	$1,100
Less depreciation	$800	$0
Income from the investment (pre-tax cash-flow minus depreciation)	$80	na
Income tax (20%)	$16	na
Consumption tax (20%)	na	$220
After-tax consumption (pre-tax cash-flow minus tax)	$864	$880
After-tax rate of return on investment*	8%	10%

na = not applicable.

* The after-tax rate of return on investment is equal to: [(consumption in year 2/consumption forgone in year 1) - 1].

Source: U.S. Department of the Treasury, Office of Tax Analysis.

Because a BAT does not allow businesses to deduct labor compensation, a BAT would add several percentage points to the tax rate on labor income. Thus, the economic benefits of greater capital formation would be offset to some extent by the reduction in labor supply caused by the higher tax rate on labor income. After accounting for the wage-increasing effect of a larger stock of capital and the wage-decreasing effect of a higher tax rate on wages, on net, the after-tax wage rate falls slightly under a BAT in the Treasury Department simulations. However, the tax on the return to saving discourages working to finance future consumption, and so induces taxpayers to work too little. By lowering the tax on future consumption, a BAT's reduction in the tax rate on capital income could help to push down the overall lifetime tax burden on labor.

Second, a broad-based BAT would tax business activity more uniformly throughout the economy. The current taxes on business income distort the allocation of capital throughout the economy because they do not impose the same tax burden on all sources of capital. Tangible business capital (e.g., equipment, buildings) is unevenly taxed while owner-occupied housing and intangible capital (e.g., patents, trademarks) are generally not taxed at all or at very low effective rates. Current law's tax differentials encourage over-investment in low-tax assets and activities at the expense of more productive investments in high-tax assets. This reduces the value of the output produced with our nation's stock of capital because taxes, rather than economic fundamentals, affect investment choices.

The more uniform treatment under a broad-based BAT would reduce a number of existing tax distortions that interfere with efficient consumption and investment decisions. However, narrowing of a BAT base through various special tax provisions, such as exemptions for food and drugs, would undermine the economic benefits of a BAT by reintroducing tax distortions.

The current tax system also distorts a number of consumption choices. For example, the value of fringe benefits, such as employer-provided health care, is excluded from an employee's taxable income. In contrast, cash wages are generally taxable. The tax advantage of such fringe benefits over cash wages induces workers to over-consume fringe benefits and to under-consume other goods and services. Under a BAT, these tax distortions would be reduced because fringe benefits would not be deductible.

It is commonly noted that consumption taxes place a tax burden on the value of wealth that exists at the time the consumption tax is imposed. The tax on wealth is unavoidable and so does not distort economic decisions. The tax occurs because the expensing of investment under a consumption tax reduces the value of old capital relative to new investment. Once the consumption tax is in place, all old capital would be worth less than an equally productive amount of new investment. The intuition is that old capital has already received the tax benefit from expensing, and has had its tax basis reduced accordingly, but must compete with new capital that has not been expensed. Consequently, old capital is worth less than new capital.[25] One particular aspect of the reduction in the value of old relative to new capital is that a consumption tax would reduce the value of assets in place at the time the consumption tax went into effect.

Compared to a world without the consumption tax, the value of old capital, including capital in place at the time of the tax change, would be reduced in proportion to the consumption tax rate.

However, because under the BAT approach business income taxes would be replaced, the net effect on asset values must include not only the effects of the BAT, but also any effects from repealing business income taxes. It is important to note that current law business income taxes are not pure income taxes, which would have no effect on asset values. Instead, business income taxes under current law are hybrids of income and consumption taxes and have some degree of expensing that already reduces the value of old capital relative to new investment. Consequently, repealing business income taxes would raise the value of existing assets. The net effect on asset values depends on whether repealing business income taxes would raise asset values by a greater or lesser extent than imposing the BAT would lower asset values. Because the BAT tax rate is so low (roughly 5 percent to 6 percent), it seems likely that in some cases the net effect would be a negligible change or possibly an increase in value.[26] Thus, it is not clear that the BAT approach discussed in this chapter would lower asset values, which might mitigate the need for transition relief to address the impact on the value of existing assets.

Nevertheless, in certain cases transition relief may be viewed as desirable to address possible windfall losses associated with the loss of existing tax attributes. For example, unused net operating losses or credits accumulated prior to enactment of a BAT could be phased out over a specified time period. Although transition relief can be provided with a view toward avoiding large

---

[25] Focusing on capital in place at the time of the tax change, this effect is perhaps most clearly seen by noting that this stock of capital is not allowed to be expensed (assuming no transition relief), but nonetheless the taxpayer has a zero basis. If the asset were sold, say for $100, the full proceeds would be subject to tax, so that the business owner would be left with only $80 after taxes, assuming a 20 percent consumption tax rate. For a new asset, the tax savings from expensing would offset in present value the tax paid on the investment's cash flow (including any tax paid on the sale of the asset). So the old asset would be worth 20 percent less that an equivalently productive new asset.

[26] Indeed, some rough estimates suggest that a BAT actually could raise the value of assets in aggregate. For example, Auerbach (1996) estimates that the consumption tax aspects of current law cause corporate assets to sell at about an 8 percent discount relative to new assets and non-corporate assets to sell at about a 6 percent discount. If these estimates proved accurate, a BAT at a 5 percent or 6 percent rate would cause a small net increase in asset values in the aggregate.

changes in wealth, allowing transition relief would increase the cost of the approach and require a higher BAT rate, which would reduce a BAT's economic benefits. Nonetheless, it is important to note that if transition relief were financed by a higher BAT rate imposed over a fixed period of time (e.g., five or ten years), then transition relief would have no effect on the GDP and other benefits of a BAT in the long run.

Inefficiencies and Distortions Created by Replacing Business Taxes with a BAT

Repealing business income taxes and imposing a BAT while retaining an individual income tax would create some inefficiencies and distortions. This section considers such inefficiencies and also potential distortions that would arise from a BAT that fails to cover all consumer goods and services, exempts small businesses and continues to require income to be calculated for certain purposes.

Repealing the corporate income tax while retaining the individual income tax creates an incentive for individual taxpayers to accumulate passive investment income in the corporate form to defer paying tax on dividends, capital gains, and interest. Special rules to deal with these situations, such as the personal holding company tax and the accumulated earnings tax under present law, may be necessary, but could also introduce complexity.[27]

Another issue is how the income of flow-though business entities, such as limited liability corporations, S corporations, partnerships, and sole proprietorships, would be treated under the BAT approach. Unlike C corporations,[28] the income of flow-through entities would be taxable under the individual income tax when it is earned. To provide the same tax treatment for income earned by flow-through entities and income earned by C corporations, flow-through businesses could be treated as separate entities subject to the same rules as C corporations.

---

[27] The personal holding company tax was enacted when the highest corporate tax rate was lower than the highest individual income tax rate. This provision of current law is intended to prevent individuals from establishing a corporation to receive and hold investment income so that it would not be taxed at higher individual income tax rates. The tax is 15 percent of undistributed personal holding company income. The accumulated earnings tax applies if a corporation is formed or used to avoid personal income tax on its shareholders by accumulating earnings and profits rather than distributing them. The accumulated earnings tax rate is 15 percent of the accumulated earnings. These taxes are in addition to any regular income tax.

[28] C corporations are entities that are subject to the corporate income tax under current law.

Alternatively, if flow-through businesses were not required to be treated as C corporations, flow-through entities with positive income would have an incentive to elect to be treated as C corporations for tax purposes, because they would be exempt from income tax until that income is paid to the owners and taxed at the individual level.[29] However, flow-through businesses with losses from their business operations might choose to maintain their flow-through status. Because the individual income tax would be retained under the BAT approach, the business loss of a flow-through entity would be deductible from the owner's personal income (such as wages) in computing taxable income, as is the case under current individual income tax rules. In contrast, the owner of a C corporation is not allowed (nor would he be allowed under the BAT approach) to deduct the corporation's loss for individual income tax purposes. To help ensure the same treatment of operating losses for owners of flow-through businesses and C corporations, rules would be needed to prevent flow-through businesses that do not elect to be treated as C corporations from using business losses to offset ordinary income. Further, rules would be needed to determine how business losses would be treated for taxpayers with multiple business interests.

Under a BAT approach, business entities (C corporations and entities treated as C corporations) would have an incentive to minimize the compensation paid to an owner for his own labor services because the owner's labor income would be taxable when it is received at individual income tax rates, and the business entity would not be permitted to deduct compensation payments. To the extent labor income is characterized as capital income and deferred, the Social Security and Medicare Trust Funds also would be affected. Rules requiring reasonable labor compensation would need to be retained, or even strengthened, to address this issue.[30]

Additional issues arise from the imposition of a BAT.[31] Although a BAT is intended to apply equally to sales of goods and services by all business entities,

---

[29] Under the existing "check the box" regulations, entities other than corporations are generally allowed to elect corporate tax treatment. Business entities that are sole proprietorships, partnerships or limited liability companies under state law are allowed to be treated as C corporations (and subject to an entity level tax) or, if they meet the eligibility criteria, as S corporations (not subject to an entity level tax).

[30] Under current law, reasonable compensation rules are in place to prevent S corporations from paying owner-employees too little as wages in order to avoid payroll taxes. The rules are also in place to prevent C corporations from paying owner-employees too much compensation in order to reduce corporate income taxes.

[31] Note that these issues may also arise if, instead of replacing the corporate income tax, a BAT were added to the current income tax system.

certain services provided to consumers, such as financial services, would be difficult to tax under a BAT. Member countries of the Organisation for Economic Co-operation and Development (OECD) generally exempt financial services under their VATs because of the difficulty of determining the value added in financial intermediation. Although a BAT can be imposed on financial services that are fee-based, such as safety deposit boxes, it is much more difficult to impose tax when the charge for the service is contained in the margin between the return paid to lenders and the amount charged to borrowers. Taxing financial services on a cash-flow basis is one approach, but that would create considerable complexity by requiring a different set of rules for financial services.[32] Further, a BAT would entail difficult line-drawing as corporations would have to distinguish between the value added of real and financial transactions that are coupled, such as the purchase of a car financed by the seller.

If only larger businesses are subject to a BAT (i.e., only businesses with sales above a certain threshold must charge BAT), then larger businesses might have an incentive to outsource work to exempt small businesses. Under a BAT, wages paid to employees would not be deductible, but fees paid to third parties, including possibly exempt small businesses, would be deductible, potentially leading to opportunities for tax planning. Rules to deal with this issue might be necessary and introduce additional complexity for businesses.

Replacing business income taxes with a BAT would impose new burdens on businesses without fully relieving them of pre-existing tax compliance burdens. The retention of investor-level taxes under the individual income tax would require businesses to continue to calculate income in order to distinguish between dividends and the return of the investor's capital, because dividends and capital gains would continue to be taxable at the individual shareholder level, whereas the return of capital would not be taxable. Moreover, businesses would also have to comply with the new BAT.

Concerns about Growth of a BAT

Some have asserted that VATs, particularly if initially imposed at low rates, could be increased and, over time, lead to the growth in federal outlays as a share of GDP. This view is based, in part, on the following premises. First, because a VAT base is large, small increases in the VAT tax rate can generate large

---

[32] For a more detailed discussion of the treatment of financial intermediaries under a VAT, see Barham, Poddar and Whalley (1987), Poddar and English (1997), and Zee (2005).

amounts of revenue. Second, depending on how a VAT is administered, it could be perceived as an invisible tax if collected from businesses rather the households.[33] Third, because a VAT is a relatively economically efficient way to collect revenue, it is less costly to the economy to expand a VAT to finance a larger federal government.

There are relatively few empirical studies on the relationship between the adoption of a VAT and the growth of government spending.[34] The empirical research, for example, has not been able to adequately address the direction of causality between the tax structure and the size of government. Casual empiricism suggests that countries without VATs, such as the United States, have smaller government sectors than countries with a VAT. More careful empirical work that controls for other factors that influence the relationship between the size of government and the presence of a VAT yield mixed results. The evidence is inconclusive on whether a VAT would facilitate the growth of government and well-known tax authorities disagree.[35]

D. DISTRIBUTIONAL ISSUES

Broad-based consumption taxes, such as a VAT, are commonly criticized for being regressive. The extent to which this criticism is accurate depends on several factors including, for example, whether households are classified according to annual income, lifetime income, or annual consumption, assumptions regarding who bears the corporate income tax, and the extent to which economic behavior changes in response to imposing a VAT.

In distributional analyses, when households are classified as rich or poor according to a broad measure of annual income, a VAT is generally found to be regressive because annual consumption falls as a percentage of annual income as annual income increases.[36] This method of classifying households' ability to pay is common because it is convenient and has intuitive appeal, and because determining alternative, simple, and explainable classifications has proven

---

[33] Of course, sales receipts to consumers could be required to separately list the VAT collected on the sale.
[34] See, for example, Becker and Mulligan (2003).
[35] Tait (1988), Stockfisch (1985) suggest that a VAT would not increase the size of the government sector, but McClure (1983) suggests that it would increase the size of the government sector.
[36] For example, see Congressional Budget Office (1992). See also Feenberg, Mitrusi and Poterba (1997) and Mieszkowski and Palumbo (2002).

difficult. It is used in the Treasury Department's distributional analysis of a BAT that is discussed below. Nonetheless, it is important to keep in mind that using annual-income measures can provide an incomplete and perhaps somewhat misleading metric of whether a household is "rich" or "poor."[37]

A conceptually preferable alternative to annual income is lifetime income, which gives a comprehensive measure of an individual's ability to pay taxes over his entire economic life. A lifetime perspective is important because a household's income can change from year to year. For example, most individuals' or households' lifetime earnings histories follow a hump-shaped pattern. Households in the lower annual income brackets contain not only those who are perennially poor, but also those who are temporarily poor due to unemployment or illness, those who are young but have high potential lifetime earnings (e.g., those just entering the work force), and those who are retired and are wealthy but have low incomes. Moreover, households tend to smooth consumption between low and high earnings periods. Therefore, some studies use annual consumption as a measure of well being.[38] Studies find that a VAT remains regressive when households are classified according to lifetime income, but the extent of the regressivity diminishes significantly.[39]

Most conventional distributional analyses of VATs also do not take into account that VATs continue to tax a significant portion of the return to investment – the supra-normal return. Recognizing that both income taxes and VATs tax a significant portion of the return to investment can also change the distributional effects of a VAT in ways that are not considered in most distributional analyses, including those that the Treasury Department prepared for this chapter, and that are discussed in more detail in Box 2.2 below.

Another factor that influences the progressivity of replacing business income taxes with a BAT is one's view regarding who bears the burden of the corporate income tax and personal taxes imposed on business income.[40] For decades it has been clearly understood that the corporate income tax is not borne exclusively by corporate shareholders, but is borne by households more generally. Consumers, workers, and owners of other types of capital all may bear the corporate income tax through higher prices, lower real wages, or lower returns, respectively. The extent to which the corporate tax is shifted from

---

[37] See, for example, Poterba (1989).
[38] When ability to pay is measured by annual consumption, then by definition the burden of a broad-based VAT is proportional.
[39] Casperson and Metcalf (1994).
[40] This issue is particularly relevant to an approach that entails replacing current business income taxes with a BAT.

corporate equity owners to other economic actors depends on the details of the tax system, how the revenue from the tax is spent, the degree to which various economic actors respond to tax prices, the time frame of the analysis, and the details of the economy. Consequently, it has proven difficult to determine, precisely, who bears the burden of the corporate income tax.

Research dating back to the early 1960s suggested that the corporate income tax might primarily be borne by owners of capital as the corporate income tax lowers the returns to all types of capital, not just capital used in the corporate sector. Capital shifts out of the corporate sector in response to the lower after-tax return offered by corporations. This research, however, assumed a fixed capital stock reflecting the dominant position of the United States in world capital markets at the time. If the capital stock varies either because of international capital flows or a savings response, the corporate tax (and, more generally, business taxes) may more easily be shifted to labor.

While there remains uncertainty in this area of research, there is increasing evidence that suggests that the corporate income tax may be borne not entirely (or even principally) by owners of capital, but instead a substantial portion of the tax may be shifted onto workers, affecting their wages and living standards. Globalization plays a role. In an open economy, with mobile capital, but immobile labor, a source-based tax like the corporate income tax could well be paid in large part by domestic labor. The intuition is simple: the incidence of a tax will generally fall on the input that is least mobile. In an international setting, where capital increasingly flows freely across borders, but labor is considerably less mobile, much of the corporate income tax will be borne by labor through lower real wages. This occurs because as capital flows out of the country, capital formation declines. As labor has less capital with which to work, labor productivity falls, which translates into lower living standards than would otherwise have occurred.

The extent to which domestic labor bears a burden depends on the degree to which investment is internationally mobile and the extent to which the United States has the power to shift some of the corporate tax burden abroad by influencing the terms of international trade in its favor. One recent study, for example, finds that U.S. labor may bear as much as 70 percent of the corporate income tax burden when capital is perfectly mobile and the country lacks the ability to shift any of the burden abroad by improving the international terms of trade.[41] That study and another recent study[42] find that labor's burden is reduced when capital mobility is

---

[41] Randolph (2006).
[42] Gravelle and Smetters (2006).

less than perfect or the United States has the power to affect the prices of traded goods and services produced in the corporate sectors.[43]

In several recent papers, empirical research focusing on the relationship between cross-country variation in corporate taxes and wages finds that labor bears a substantial portion of the corporate income tax.[44] Again, the mechanism is less capital investment, which reduces labor productivity and, ultimately, living standards. While corporate tax rates change infrequently within a single country, many countries have had major corporate tax reforms over the last 25 years. These papers use these reforms to estimate the effects of corporate taxation. Whether these results, which may have been derived to some extent from the changes in tax rates among smaller economies, can be applied directly to the United States is an open question. Nevertheless, this empirical research suggests a link between corporate taxes and wages.

Even without international capital flows, prominent economic models suggest that changes in the level of domestic savings may also result in a shift of much of the burden of the corporate tax onto labor. In these models, the corporate tax lowers the return to saving, which causes households to save less, which lowers the capital stock, which in turn reduces labor productivity and real wages. Both of the most commonly used theoretical economic models of the effects of taxes on household decisions about working, saving, and consuming suggest that a large fraction of the corporate tax is likely shifted onto labor.[45] Of course, the actual degree of shifting depends on the extent to which savings is responsive to changes in taxes, a subject on which there is considerable uncertainty.[46] Nevertheless, these models are highly suggestive that the burden of the corporate income tax shifts in large part to labor.

---

[43] Analyses of the incidence of the corporate tax that focus on international capital flows often assume that other countries do not change their corporate taxes in response to a change in the U.S. corporate tax. Under that assumption, for example, if the United States reduced its corporate tax rate and other countries did not change their corporate tax rates, the United States would attract more capital and labor would benefit from higher wages. However, if other countries responded to the U.S. rate reduction by reducing their tax rates, capital inflows might be more modest and capital would be likely to bear more of the corporate income tax.

[44] Arulampalam, Devereux, and Maffini (2007), Hassett and Mathur (2006), and Felix (2007).

[45] Auerbach and Kotlikoff (1987) and Judd (2006).

[46] Bernheim (2002).

Table 2.3. Distribution of the Federal Tax Burden Under Current Law and a Business Activities Tax With Two Assumptions on the Incidence of the Corporate Income Tax

		Percent of Federal Taxes Paid		
First Quintile	0.3	0.5	0.4	0.5
Second Quintile	2.1	3.0	2.5	3.0
Third Quintile	8.0	9.7	8.7	9.7
Fourth Quintile	17.9	20.1	18.7	20.1
Fifth Quintile	71.5	66.6	69.6	66.6
Bottom 50%	5.5	7.4	6.3	7.4
Top 10%	54.9	48.3	52.2	48.3
Top 5%	42.0	34.4	38.9	34.4
Top 1%	23.4	16.4	20.5	16.4

Note: Estimates of 2015 law at 2007 cash income levels. Quintiles begin at cash income of: Second $13,310; Third $28,507; Fourth $50,448; Highest $87,758; Top 10% $128,676; Top 5% $177,816; Top 1% $432,275; Bottom 50% below $38,255.

*The Administration's policy baseline is similar to current law but assumes permanent extension of the 2001 and 2003 tax relief.

Source: U.S. Department of the Treasury, Office of Tax Analysis.

To reflect these differing views and build on the recent research, the Treasury Department prepared two sets of distributional analyses for replacement of business income taxes with a BAT (table 2.3). In the first set of distributional analysis (columns 1 and 2), the traditional assumption employed by the Treasury Department – that the corporate income tax is borne entirely by owners of capital – is used. In the second set of distributional analysis (columns 3 and 4), the Treasury Department prepared tables that assume labor bears 70 percent of the corporate income tax. This analysis is consistent with one recent study,[47] but perhaps more conservative than the recent trio of empirical papers discussed above. In both analyses, the BAT is distributed to the income sources – capital and labor.

Two conclusions can be drawn from table 2.3. First, replacing business income taxes with a BAT tends to reduce the share of federal taxes paid by higher income taxpayers regardless of how much of the corporate income tax is

---

[47] Randolph (2006).

borne by labor. Second, replacing business income taxes with a BAT is substantially less regressive when the current corporate income tax is assumed to be borne substantially by labor. The increase in the share of federal taxes paid by the bottom four quintiles (i.e., families with incomes up to $87,758) is only 3.0 percentage points rather than 5.0 percentage points when labor is assumed to bear 70 percent of the current corporate income tax.

> Box 2.2: Distributional Effects of Taxing Consumption
>
> It is sometimes suggested that a consumption tax is less fair than an income tax because the benefit of not taxing capital income accrues disproportionately to those with higher incomes. As has been noted, consumption taxes are generally less regressive from a lifetime perspective than an annual perspective. Consumption taxes may also be less regressive than often thought because a consumption tax and income tax base both include key elements of capital income. This point runs counter to conventional distributional analyses of consumption taxes, which broadly conclude that the major difference between a consumption and income tax is that the former imposes no tax on capital income.
>
> Capital income can be decomposed into four components: (1) the return to waiting (i.e., the opportunity cost of capital), (2) the return to risk taking (i.e., the risk premium for investing), (3) economic profit (i.e., the infra-marginal return to investing), and (4) the difference between expected and actual returns. The key to analyzing the different distributional effects of a consumption tax base and an income tax base is that a consumption tax exempts the first component of capital income – the return to waiting or opportunity cost of capital – from tax, while it is included under an income tax. The three remaining components – sometimes referred to as the "supra-normal" return – are taxed under both a consumption and income tax.
>
> To understand how a consumption tax subjects to tax some capital income, it is useful to consider exactly how the tax treats investment expenditures. Under a BAT, for example, a firm expenses its capital purchases. A successful investment generates a series of future cash flows to the firm. These future cash flows will be subject to tax, but the present value of the expected future series of tax liabilities using the opportunity cost of funds (e.g., the Treasury bill rate) will exactly equal the tax value of expensing the capital expenditure. What is important to

recognize is that to the extent the future cash flows from the investment exceed (in present value) the initial investment, the excess (or supra-normal return) will be subject to tax under either an income or consumption tax.

The general public can be viewed as a proportional shareholder in all enterprises – a co-investor – under both an income tax or consumption tax. The public, in effect, shares in the rewards and risks to the extent returns are unusually high or low. Only the return to waiting or what economists call the opportunity cost of capital is exempt from tax under a consumption tax. Whether this distinction is important depends critically on how large the opportunity cost of capital is in relation to total capital income and who tends to receive this component of capital income.

How important the appropriate conceptual treatment of supra-normal returns is to the distribution of the tax burden under a BAT is largely an empirical question. Gentry and Hubbard (1997) found that replacing the current income tax with a consumption tax would be considerably less regressive than conventional analysis would indicate when the analysis recognized that the consumption tax would collect tax on supra-normal returns. In contrast, Cronin, Nunns, and Toder (1996) found that accounting for supra- normal returns made little difference.

E. BORDER TAX ADJUSTMENTS AND INTERNATIONAL TRADE

VATs (of which a BAT is one type) are typically levied on a destination basis, in which goods are taxed according to where they are consumed. Alternatively, a VAT can be levied on an origin basis, in which goods are taxed according to where they are produced.

An origin-based BAT taxes exports but not imports, and a destination-based BAT taxes imports but not exports. Border tax adjustments, which refund the accumulated BAT on goods that are exported and impose BAT on imports as if they were produced domestically, are needed to remove the tax on exports and impose the tax on imports under a destination-based BAT. Applying a BAT on a destination-basis and implementing border tax adjustments ensures that businesses may only claim deductions that are offset by corresponding inclusions. Closing the system in this way helps prevent tax evasion through cross-border transactions structured to generate tax deductions for payments to foreign parties.

Border tax adjustments are commonly perceived as providing a trade advantage, although many argue that adjustments do not improve the balance of trade in the aggregate.[48] Any apparent cost advantage would be offset by differences in the real price level across nations as reflected through changes in exchange rates or in other prices. These price adjustments work over time to negate any permanent improvement in competitiveness. There could, however, be effects on specific sectors or industries within the economy.

To illustrate the argument that border tax adjustments do not improve the balance of trade, consider a simple example.[49] Assume that the United States imposes a 25- percent origin-based tax and that it exports 100 of X-goods at $10 each and imports from Europe 100 of M-goods at $10 each. Trade is balanced, exports and imports equal $1,000, and the exchange rate is €1 per dollar. U.S. producers charge $10 for each X-good and clear $8 after tax. European producers charge €10 for each M-good exported to the United States and clear €10.

Assume that the United States decides to border-adjust its tax system and imposes a 25-percent tax on imports and rebates the 25-percent tax previously imposed on exports. With the border adjustment, exports are tax free. As a result, U.S. producers need to charge only $8 for each X-good to receive $8, while European producers need to charge €12.5 to receive €10 for each M-good exported to the United States. If exchange rates did not change, the lower price for U.S. exports would increase the number of X- goods purchased abroad and the higher price for M-goods would reduce imports purchased by Americans. However, this situation cannot persist indefinitely because the number of dollars demanded by Europeans would have increased (because Europeans will desire more X-goods) while the number of dollars supplied by Americans would have fallen (because Americans will desire less M-goods).

To restore balance in the foreign exchange market, the value of the dollar must rise by 25 percent to €1.25. At the new exchange rate, the number of dollars demanded and supplied return to balance. U.S. producers charge $8 for X-goods, which translates to €10 at the new exchange rate and exports of X-goods stay at their original level. European producers charge €12.5 for M-goods sold in the United States, which translates to $10 at the new exchange rate, and U.S. imports remain at their original level. Absent flexible exchange rates, the real price level across nations would still adjust to achieve the same result, although the

---

[48] Congressional Budget Office (1992) and Joint Committee on Taxation (1991).
[49] See Viard (2004).

adjustment process might well take longer. Through the adjustment process, trade would ultimately be unaffected by the border adjustments.[50]

F. SIMPLICITY AND ENFORCEABILITY

Like other taxes, a BAT would impose compliance costs on businesses that are required to calculate and pay it and administrative costs on the federal government to operate and enforce it. Some countries have encountered significant cases of evasion or fraud in the operation of their VATs, particularly with respect to VAT refunds.[51]

Several studies have estimated the federal government's administrative costs and businesses' compliance costs for a hypothetical VAT in the United States. Administrative and compliance costs of a VAT depend heavily on design features, such as whether there are multiple rates and the sales threshold for registration. The Treasury Department has previously estimated that the administrative costs of a credit-method VAT would be about $700 million per year when fully phased in, while other studies indicate that the administrative costs may be as high as $2.3 billion.[52]

The Congressional Budget Office estimated that the annual cost for businesses of complying with a VAT with a $25,000 small business exemption would have been from $4 billion to $7 billion in 1988.[53] About 90 percent of the cost would have been incurred by businesses with sales under $1 million.[54] These estimates suggest that a BAT may have a large potential compliance cost saving compared to the present business income taxes, which are estimated to be roughly $40

---

[50] This conclusion depends on all goods and services being taxed equally. If exemptions are introduced, the impact on the trade balance will depend on tax rates applied to the imported or exported goods and services.

[51] Decisions regarding BAT exemptions, thresholds, and zero-rating would affect the likelihood of fraudulent claims (Keen and Smith (2007)).

[52] U.S. Department of the Treasury (1984). The Congressional Budget Office (1992) estimated that the administrative costs would have been about $750 million to $1.5 billion in 1988. The General Accounting Office (1993) estimated that the administrative costs of a broad-based VAT would be $1.8 billion per year when fully phased in. These costs were estimated to decrease to $1.4 billion per year with a $25,000 small business exemption, and $1.2 billion per year with a $100,000 exemption. The IRS (1993) estimated that the administrative cost of a VAT with a $100,000 exemption would be $2.3 billion in the second year of full implementation.

[53] Congressional Budget Office (1992).

[54] In addition to these U.S. studies, a recent study for the United Kingdom estimated that the burden of preparing and filing VAT returns costs £170 per registered business (£120 million per year for 1.8 million registered businesses). See HM Revenue and Customs (2006).

billion annually.⁵⁵ However, as noted above, the extent to which business compliance costs would decrease depends upon the particular features of a BAT. In addition, some of the apparent cost saving from replacing business income taxes with a BAT may not occur if states retain their business income tax systems.⁵⁶

Further, as noted above, with a BAT that retains the individual income tax system, the benefits of replacing business income taxes with a single rate broad-based BAT would be counteracted to some extent because businesses would continue to have to determine income in order to distinguish between dividends and capital gains (which would be taxable at the individual level) from returns of the investor's capital (which would not be taxable).

G. IMPLICATIONS FOR STATE AND LOCAL GOVERNMENTS

Another effect of eliminating the federal corporate income tax would be the effect on the ability of states to administer their current business income taxes. Many states with business income taxes generally conform to the federal tax system and rely heavily on federal definitions of income and deductions. In addition, states build upon the federal structure of definitions and regulations, information reporting, and tax withholding. Without that structure, it would be extremely difficult for states to maintain their existing business income tax systems, and if they did maintain them, the simplicity gains from eliminating the federal business income taxes could be eroded.

State and local governments also would be faced with the prospect of conforming their tax bases to the federal base, including both their retail sales taxes and state corporate income taxes. Deviations from the federal base would increase firms' compliance costs. If state and local governments primarily raise revenue by piggybacking on a federal BAT, tax rates could rise to a level that would make enforcement more difficult. On the other hand, to the extent state and local governments conform to a federal BAT, enforcement difficulties could be reduced.

---

⁵⁵ This compliance cost estimate includes both corporate and non-corporate businesses.
⁵⁶ Slemrod and Bakija (1996).

H. VATs in Other Countries

Over 140 countries have VATs. Twenty-nine of the 30 OECD countries have VATs. The United States is the exception, although most states impose a retail sales tax.

There are major differences in the rates and structures of the VATs in OECD countries (table 2.4). The average standard VAT rate for OECD countries is 17.6 percent, but ranges from 5 percent (Japan) to 25 percent (Denmark, Norway, and Sweden). Six of the 29 OECD countries have standard VAT rates under 15 percent (Australia, Canada, Japan, Korea, New Zealand, and Switzerland). The remaining 23 countries have standard rates between 15 percent and 25 percent. Many countries also have reduced rates or zero rates. Reduced rates generally apply to basic essentials (e.g., medical and hospital care, food and water supplies), certain utilities (e.g., public transport, postal services, and public television), and certain socially desirable activities (e.g., charitable services, culture, and sports). Under zero rates (such as for exports), no tax is levied on the good or service and credit for VAT paid is allowed.

In addition to reduced or zero rates, countries also provide VAT exemptions (i.e., sales are not taxed but VAT paid on purchases from other businesses is not recovered). Most OECD countries exempt sectors that are viewed as important for social reasons, such as health, education, and charities. Most countries also exempt certain sectors for practical reasons. Financial and insurance services are generally exempt because of the practical difficulties in determining the tax base. In addition, those services may be subject to specific taxes. Other activities that are sometimes exempt include postal services, letting of immovable property, and the supply of land and buildings.

Approximately two-thirds of OECD countries offer exemptions for small businesses to reduce administrative and compliance costs. Businesses with sales below a specified threshold generally are not required to register for the VAT (table 2.4). The threshold for exemption varies considerably, ranging from approximately $2,400 (Iceland) to $93,700 (United Kingdom). Ten countries have thresholds below $25,000 (Austria, Canada, Denmark, Finland, Germany, Greece, Iceland, Luxembourg, Norway, and Poland), and nine countries have thresholds of $25,000 or more (Australia, Czech Republic, France, Ireland, Japan, New Zealand, Slovak Republic, Switzerland, and the United Kingdom). Ten OECD countries report no general exemption threshold (Belgium, Hungary, Italy, Korea, Mexico, Netherlands, Portugal, Spain, Sweden, and Turkey).

Table 2.4. VAT Rates and Structure in OECD Countries*

Country	Standard Rate	Reduced Rate	Domestic Zero Rate **	Threshold $ U.S.
Australia	10.0	-	yes	36,496
Austria	20.0	10.0 and 12.0	no	24,229
Belgium	21.0	6 and 12.0	yes	-
Canada	7.0	-	yes	23,622
Czech Republic	19.0	5	no	68,439
Denmark	25.0	-	yes	5,910
Finland	22.0	8.0 and 17.0	yes	9,081
France	19.6	2.0 and 5.5	no	85,061
Germany	16.0	7	no	18,637
Greece	19.0	4.5 and 9.0	no	12,912
Hungary	20.0	5 and 15	no	-
Iceland	24.5	14	yes	2,442
Ireland	21.0	4.8 and 13.5	yes	50,495
Italy	20.0	4.0 and 10.0	yes	-
Japan	5.0	-	no	75,188
Korea	10.0	-	yes	-
Luxembourg	15.0	3.0, 6.0 and 12.0	no	10,163
Mexico	15.0		yes	-
Netherlands	19.0	6	no	-
New Zealand	12.5	-	yes	26,846
Norway	25.0	8.0 and 13.0	yes	5,274
Poland	22.0	7	yes	10,580
Portugal	21.0	5.0 and 12.0	no	-
Slovak Republic	19.0		no	87,209
Spain	16.0	4.0 and 7.0	no	-
Sweden	25.0	6.0 and 12.0	yes	-

Table 2.4. (Continued).

Country	Standard Rate	Reduced Rate	Domestic Zero Rate **	Threshold $ U.S.
Switzerland	7.6	2.4 and 3.6	yes	42,373
Turkey	18.0	1.0 and 8.0	no	-
United Kingdom	17.5	5	yes	93,700
Unweighted Average	17.6			

*The standard rate applies to 2006. Information on reduced rates, domestic zero rates and thresholds applies to 2005.
** Domestic zero rate means tax is applied at a rate of zero to certain domestic sales. It does not include zero rated exports.
Sources: OECD, *Consumption Tax Trends*, 2006, and the OECD Tax Database at www.OECD.org

REFERENCES

Arulampalam, Wiji, Michael P. Devereux, and Giorgia Maffini. 2007. "The Incidence of Corporate Income Tax on Wages," Mimeo, University of Warwick, September.

Auerbach, Alan J. 1996. "Tax Reform, Capital Allocation, Efficiency and Growth." In *Economic Effects of Fundamental Tax Reform,* eds. Henry J. Aaron and William G. Gale, 2-73. Washington, DC: The Brookings Institution.

Auerbach, Alan J. and Roger H. Gordon. 2002. "Taxation of Financial Services Under A VAT." *American Economic Review* 92(2): 411-416.

Auerbach, Alan J. and Laurence J. Kotlikoff. 1987. *Dynamic Fiscal Policy,* New York, NY: Cambridge University Press.

Barham, Vicky, Satya N. Poddar and John Whalley. 1987. "The Tax Treatment of Insurance under a Consumption Type, Destination Basis VAT." *National Tax Journal* 40(2): 171-182.

Becker, Gary S. and Casey B. Mulligan. 2003. "Deadweight Costs and the Size of Government." *Journal of Law and Economics* 46: 293-340.

Bernheim, B. Douglas. 2002. "A Note on Dynamic Tax Incidence." *The Distribution of Tax Burdens, 2003*. Elgar Reference Collection. International Library of Critical Writings in Economics, vol. 155, 474-492. Cheltenham, U.K. and Northampton, Mass.

Bradford, David F. 1986. *Untangling the Income Tax.* Cambridge, MA: Harvard University Press.

Casperson, Eric and Gilbert Metcalf. 1994. "Is a Value Added Tax Regressive? Annual Versus Lifetime Incidence Measures." *National Tax Journal* 47(4): 731-746.

Congressional Budget Office. 1992. *Effects of Adopting a Value-Added Tax.* Washington, DC: Congressional Budget Office.

Cronin, Julie-Anne, James Nunns and Eric Toder. 1996. "Distributional Effects of Recent Tax Reform Proposals." Unpublished manuscript.

Feenberg, Daniel, Andrew Mitrusi and James Poterba. 1997. "Distributional Effects of Adopting a National Retail Sales Tax." In *Tax Policy and the Economy*, ed. James Porterba, Vol. 11, 49-89. Cambridge, MA: The MIT Press.

Felix, R. Alison. 2007. "Passing the Burden: Corporate Tax Incidence in Open Economies." Chapter 1, Ph.D. Dissertation, University of Michigan.

General Accounting Office. 1993. *Value-Added Tax: Administrative Costs Vary With Complexity and Number of Businesses.* GAO/GGD-93-78. Washington, DC: General Accounting Office.

Gentry, William M. and R. Glenn Hubbard. 1997. "Distributional Implications of Introducing a Broad-Based Consumption Tax." NBER Working Paper No. 5832, Cambridge, MA: National Bureau of Economic Research.

Gravelle, Jane G. and Kent A. Smetters. 2006. "Does the Open Economy Assumption Really Mean That Labor Bears the Burden of a Capital Income Tax?" *B.E. Journals in Economic Analysis and Policy: Advances in Economic Analysis and Policy* 6(1): 1-42.

Grubert, Harry and James Mackie. 2000. "Must Financial Services Be Taxed Under a Consumption Tax?" *National Tax Journal* 53(1): 23-40.

Hassett, Kevin A. and Aparna Mathur. 2006. "Taxes and Wages." American Enterprise Insitute for Public Policy Research, Working Paper Number 128, June.

HM Revenue and Customs. 2006. "Filing VAT and Company Tax Returns." Report by the Comptroller and Auditor General, HC 102 Session 2006-2007, December 13.

Internal Revenue Service. 1993. *Administrative Issues in Implementing a Federal Value Added Tax.* Washington, DC: Internal Revenue Service.

Japanese Ministry of Finance, Tax Bureau. 2005. *An Outline of Japanese Taxes.* Tokyo, Japan.

Joint Committee on Taxation. 1991. *Factors Affecting the International Competitiveness of the United States.* Washington, DC: U.S. Government Printing Office.

Judd, Kenneth L. 2001. "The Impact of Tax Reform in Modern Dynamic Economies." In *Transition Costs of Fundamental Tax Reform*, eds. Kevin A. Hassett and R. Glenn Hubbard, 5-53. Washington, DC: AEI Press.

Keen, Michael and Stephen Smith. 2007. "VAT Fraud and Evasion: What Do We Know, and What Can Be Done?" IMF Working Paper WP/07/3 1.

Lyon, Andrew B. and Peter R. Merrill. 1999. "Asset Price Effects of Fundamental Tax Reform." In *Transition Costs of Fundamental Tax Reform*, eds. Kevin A. Hassett and R. Glenn Hubbard, 58-92. Washington, DC: AEI Press.

McLure, Charles E., Jr. 1987. *The Value-Added Tax: Key to Deficit Reduction?* Washington, DC: American Enterprise Institute.

McClure, Charles E. 1983. "Value Added Tax: Has the Time Come?" In *New Directions in Federal Tax Policy for the 1980s*, eds. Charls E. Walker and Mark Bloomfield. Cambridge: Ballinger.

Mieszkowski, Peter and Michael Palumbo. 2002. "Distributive Analysis of Fundamental Tax Reform." In *United States Tax Reform in the 21st Century*, eds. George Zodrow and Peter Mieszkowski, 140-178. Cambridge: Cambridge University Press.

Organisation for Economic Co-operation and Development. 2006. *Revenue Statistics 1965 – 2005.* Paris: Organisation for Economic Co-operation and Development.

Organisation for Economic Co-operation and Development. 2006. *Consumption Tax Trends.* Paris: Organisation for Economic Co-operation and Development.

Poddar, Satya and Morley English. 1997. "Taxation of Financial Services Under a Value- Added Tax: Applying the Cash-Flow Approach." *National Tax Journal* 50(1): 89-111.

Poterba, James. 1989. "Lifetime Incidence and the Distributional Burden of Excise Taxes." *American Economic Review* 79(2): 325-330.

Randolph, William C. 2006. "International Burdens of the Corporate Income Tax." Congressional Budget Office Working Paper Series 2006-09.

Schenk, Alan. 1995. "Japanese Consumption Tax After Six Years: A Unique VAT Matures," *Tax Notes International* 11(21): 1379-1393.

Slemrod, Joel and John Bakija. 1996. *Taxing Ourselves: A Citizen's Guide to the Great Debate Over Tax Reform.* Cambridge, MA: The MIT Press.

Stockfisch, J.A. 1985. "Value-Added Taxes and the Size of Government: Some Evidence." *National Tax Journal* 38(4): 547-552.

Tait, Alan A. 1988. *Value Added Tax: International Practice and Problems.* Washington, DC: International Monetary Fund.

U.S. Department of the Treasury. 1984. *Tax Reform for Fairness, Simplicity, and Economic Growth, Vol. 3, Value-Added Tax.* Washington, DC: U.S. Department of the Treasury.

Viard, Alan D. 2001. "The Transition to Consumption Taxation, Part 2: The Impact on Existing Financial Assets." *Federal Reserve Bank of Dallas Economic and Financial Review* 2ndQ: 20-31.

Viard, Alan D. 2004. Letter to the Editor. *Tax Notes.* October 4: 122.

Zee, Howell H. 1995. "Value-Added Tax." In *Tax Policy Handbook*, ed. Parthasarathi Shome. Washington, DC: The International Monetary Fund.

Zee, Howell H. 2005. "A New Approach to Taxing Financial Intermediation Services Under a Value-Added Tax." *National Tax Journal* 5 8(1): 77-92.

Zodrow, George R. 2002. "Transitional Issues in Tax Reform." In *United States Tax Reform in the 21st Century,* ed. George Zodrow and Peter Mieszkowski, 245-283. Cambridge, MA: Cambridge University Press.

Chapter 3

BUSINESS TAX REFORM WITH BASE BROADENING/REFORM OF THE U.S. INTERNATIONAL TAX RULES

A. INTRODUCTION

The existing U.S. system of taxing capital income creates a number of distortions that interfere with the efficient and productive functioning of the U.S. economy. These distortions include: a tax disincentive to save and invest generally, caused by taxing the return earned on investment; a tax disincentive to invest in the corporate business sector, caused by the double tax on corporate profits; a tax incentive for corporations to finance with debt rather than with equity, caused by tax provisions that allow firms to deduct interest but not dividends; a tax incentive to engage in certain economic activities rather than others, caused by special tax provisions that are only selectively available; and a tax disincentive to repatriating foreign earnings. These distortions waste economic resources and lower the standard of living produced by the U.S. economy.[57]

This chapter discusses approaches for reform of business income taxation that would broaden the tax base and either lower the business tax rate or provide a faster write-off of the cost of investment. It also discusses an approach for reforming the U.S. international tax system by moving to a territorial tax system.

One approach for reforming the business tax system is to eliminate the various special business tax provisions in exchange for either lower business tax rates or

---

[57] Several of these distortions are discussed in more detail in the U.S. Department of the Treasury (2007).

faster write-off of business investment. This revenue-neutral approach would replace the vast array of special tax provisions, which are sometimes highly targeted to encourage particular economic activity, with broad tax relief for all businesses.

Lowering the tax rate on business income (including both the corporate income tax rate and the tax rate imposed on non-corporate businesses) would help to reduce all five of the distortions enumerated above. A lower tax rate would reduce the tax on the return to saving and investing in the U.S. economy, thereby promoting U.S. saving and capital formation. Importantly, a lower rate would benefit both U.S. citizens and foreign companies doing business in the United States and would make the United States a more attractive place in which to invest. Lowering the corporate tax rate, by lowering the tax rate on profits, would help to reduce the tax penalty on corporate investment and the tax incentive for corporations to finance with debt rather than with equity. A lower tax rate also would reduce the benefit conveyed by many special tax provisions, thereby reducing the economic distortions caused by these special tax provisions. Finally, a lower tax rate would reduce the residual tax on repatriated foreign earnings.

Rather than being used to lower the tax rate, the revenue from base broadening could be used to allow partial expensing. Partial expensing, by lowering the effective tax burden on business income, would in several respects have effects that are qualitatively similar to a reduction in the tax rate. Like a tax rate reduction, partial expensing would stimulate U.S. capital formation and reduce the tax penalty on business investment.

Indeed, as a policy to encourage investment, partial expensing has an advantage over tax rate reduction. The benefits of partial expensing are generally limited to new investment, whereas tax rate reduction provides a tax benefit to the return earned on new and old capital alike. Thus, partial expensing would encourage more investment per dollar of revenue spent than a tax rate reduction. Expensing also would benefit both U.S. and foreign investors alike, generally making the United States a more attractive place to locate businesses. To the extent that partial expensing is generally available for a wide variety of business investments, it would provide uniform treatment that would not encourage some types of investment over others for tax reasons. In contrast to rate reduction, however, partial expensing is unlikely to reduce the tax incentive for corporations to finance with debt rather than with equity, nor would it reduce the tax disincentive to repatriating foreign earnings.

Broadening the tax base means repealing a wide variety of special tax provisions. Such repeal would help to remove taxes from investment decisions, allowing market fundamentals to drive investors' choices. By rationalizing the tax system, base broadening would add to the benefits of rate reduction. In another sense, however, base broadening works against a reduction in the tax rate or partial expensing because repeal of special tax provisions means a higher tax burden on those investments, and hence on average for all investments in the economy. This effect makes it less likely that the combination of base broadening and, in particular, rate reduction would dramatically increase the amount of capital used in the U.S. economy. Nonetheless, in other ways the revised tax system would generally be more efficient because it would have reduced to some extent distorting tax differences across sectors, assets, and financing. In other words, the tax system would be more neutral or uniform in its treatment of income earned on alternative investments.

The size of the economic benefits achieved by revenue-neutral business tax reform is an empirical matter. Results depend on how much rate reduction or partial expensing can be achieved and on the effects of repealing specific special business tax provisions. The Treasury Department estimates that broadening the business tax base by eliminating a broad range of special tax provisions would allow the top federal business tax rate to be lowered to 28 percent or, in the alternative, would allow 35 percent of new business investment to be expensed (written off immediately), in either case without any change in total federal revenues.[58]

In the Treasury Department's economic model, the economic benefit from such a revenue neutral rate reduction appears to be relatively modest, while the economic benefit of partial expensing is somewhat larger. As discussed more completely below, negligible or small gains seem especially likely when base broadening is used to finance a lower business tax rate. This raises the question of whether such a revenue-neutral reform would allow deep enough reductions in business taxes to improve the competitiveness of U.S. businesses.

A larger tax rate reduction or greater partial expensing could potentially achieve larger economic benefits, stemming from a larger inflow of capital into the United States than the Treasury Department's economic model suggests. Such a reform could not be financed by raising other taxes on business through base broadening, and so would have to be financed in some other way (e.g., by raising non-business taxes, by borrowing, or by cutting government spending). The net benefits would ultimately depend on how business taxes were reduced (rate reduction or partial expensing) and on the details of how the tax relief was

---

[58] Lowering the top federal business tax rate to 28 percent would reduce the combined U.S. federal-state tax rate from 39 percent to 33 percent.

financed.[59] If financed by increased borrowing, for example, a reduction in business taxes, whether lower business tax rates or partial expensing, would at least partially be offset by the rise in interest rates as the extra government borrowing crowds out private investment. Nevertheless, the key point is that large reductions in U.S. business taxes (e.g., a 20-percent corporate tax rate or 65-percent expensing) could potentially produce larger economic benefits than the Treasury Department model suggests as the United States moves from its current position as a high-tax rate country to a low-tax rate country.

The tax disincentive to repatriating foreign earnings, the fifth distortion enumerated above, could be addressed by moving to a "territorial" tax system. Under current law, U.S. corporations are taxed on their worldwide income and are provided a tax credit for income taxes paid to foreign governments. This foreign tax credit is generally limited to the amount of U.S. tax that would have been incurred if the income had been earned in the United States. The foreign earnings of a subsidiary of a U.S. corporation with an active business abroad (such as a manufacturing operation) are taxed by the United States only when those active earnings are repatriated as a dividend. Under the type of territorial system used by many U.S. trading partners, some or all active overseas earnings of their businesses are exempt from taxation in the home country.

The present U.S. system for taxing the foreign source income of U.S. multinational corporations has several undesirable effects.[60] The present system distorts economic behavior. For example, corporations may forgo U.S. investment opportunities to avoid U.S. taxes. The current system also distorts the choice of where to exploit intangible assets, such as patents, and the choice of where to locate income and expenses for tax purposes. Finally, the current system is very complex, and corporations may incur planning costs to restrict their dividend repatriations from abroad.

A type of territorial system often referred to as a "dividend exemption" system would have several advantages as compared to present law. United States multinational corporations would no longer have an incentive to forgo U.S. investment opportunities to avoid U.S. tax on repatriated foreign earnings. Nor would they have to engage in elaborate tax planning to restrict such dividend repatriations.

Such a system would, however, alter the U.S. tax treatment of royalties and certain other income subject to low foreign taxes. Under present law, foreign

---

[59] For example, a 20-percent corporate tax rate or 65-percent expensing for all new business investment could be obtained at a net revenue cost of about $1.2 trillion over 10 years.

tax credits attributable to highly taxed dividends often shield royalty and other income from U.S. tax. As a result, U.S. multinational corporations may have an incentive to exploit a patent overseas rather than in the United States because the royalties paid to the U.S. parent may be largely exempt from U.S. tax.

A dividend exemption system also would raise several other concerns. U.S. multinational corporations could have a stronger incentive to shift income and assets abroad because such shifting may result in exempt foreign income. A dividend exemption system also would create incentives for tax planning to reduce allocations of expenses to exempt foreign source income. Further, although a dividend exemption system would reduce some of the complexity related to the current foreign tax credit rules, other complex provisions would remain (such as the rules for pricing transactions between related parties).

Another concern sometimes expressed about a dividend exemption system is that it would encourage investment in low-tax countries because dividends from those investments would be tax exempt in the United States. However, a dividend exemption system that eliminates the U.S. tax on dividends, but has full taxation of royalties and disallows the deduction of expenses allocated to exempt income, is likely to increase the effective tax rate on income from low-tax countries. Furthermore, lowering the tax on domestic investment income, either through rate reduction or partial expensing, would favor domestic investment over foreign investment.

In addition to addressing tax distortions, business tax reform must address U.S. competitiveness. Business tax reform discussions have frequently focused on two aspects of competitiveness: (1) the ability of U.S. companies operating abroad to compete with foreign companies, and (2) the attractiveness of the United States as a place to invest relative to other nations. Depending on their features, some types of territorial tax systems might help level the playing field between U.S. companies and their foreign competitors. However, absent any other change to the U.S. business tax system, such systems have the potential risk of making certain investments abroad more attractive in a low tax rate country relative to investment in the United States, such as an investment without significant intangibles.[61] Thus, coupling a move towards a territorial system with other changes, such as a lower business tax rate or faster write-off of business investment, could provide an approach to business tax reform that both levels

---

[60] For a detailed discussion, see Grubert and Mutti (2001), Grubert and Altshuler (forthcoming), and U.S. Department of the Treasury (2007).

[61] As discussed below, a dividend exemption system that includes full taxation of royalties and disallowance of expenses allocated to exempt income would increase the effective tax rate for a typical investment in a low-tax country.

the playing field for U.S. businesses operating abroad and, at the same time, makes the United States a more attractive place to invest. However, the reduction in U.S. business taxes required to maintain the appropriate balance between these two objectives might not be sufficiently large under a revenue-neutral business tax reform.

B. Broadening the Business Tax Base and Either Lowering the Business Tax Rate or Permitting Faster Write-off of Investment

The current business tax base includes an array of special tax provisions that reduce taxes for particular types of activities, industries, and businesses. These provisions take the form of myriad exclusions and deductions from income, preferential tax rates, income deferral, and tax credits. Most of these provisions were enacted years ago and have evolved over many decades. These special provisions generally are intended to promote activities that are claimed to have spillover effects that benefit the economy. A prominent example is the research and experimentation (R&E) tax credit. Arguably, by raising an inventor's return, it helps to correct for the inability of the inventor to reap the full rewards of his invention because of the failure of patent and other legal protections to forestall completely others from using the new idea, product, or process.

Nonetheless, to the extent special tax provisions are not well targeted, are ill defined, or simply are not effective, they may have no economic effect. Worse yet, if the subsidies are effective, and if the activities do not produce the desired spillover benefits, then these provisions lead to a misallocation of investment that reduces the productivity of the nation's stock of capital because the special provisions encourage investment decisions based on taxes, rather than on economic fundamentals.

In summary, special provisions narrow the business tax base and require that business tax rates be higher to raise the same tax revenue. As shown in table 3.1,[62]

---

[62] The table itemizes each special tax provision that, if eliminated, would raise more than $5 billion over a 10-year period, assuming business income taxes would have a comprehensive income base with the same statutory tax rates as the current system. The estimates assume no transition rules except for accelerated depreciation, which is assumed to be repealed only for investments made beginning in 2008. Unlike the analysis included in the earlier Treasury Department study, see U.S. Department of the Treasury (2007), the estimates in Table 3.1 include the effect of eliminating these special tax provisions for both corporations and flow-through

these special business tax provisions, if repealed, would result in an additional $1.3 trillion in revenue over 10 years.[63] As indicated above, repeal of all of these provisions would allow the top business tax rate (for both corporate and non-corporate businesses) to be lowered to 28 percent or, in the alternative, would allow 35 percent of new business investment, including equipment, structures, and inventories, to be written off immediately.

Table 3.1. Special Tax Provisions Subtantially Narrow the Business Tax Base

	Revenue, 2008-2017 (FY)		
	Corporate	Non-Corporate	Total
Major Special Business Tax Provisions		$ billions	
Deduction for U.S. production/manufacturing activities	210	48	258
Research and experimentation (R&E) tax credit	132	1	133
Low income housing tax credit	55	6	61
Exclusion of interest on life insurance savings	30	0	30
Inventory property sales source rules	29	0	29
Deductibility of charitable contributions	28	0	28
Special ESOP rules	23	4	27
Exemption of credit union income	19	0	19
New technology credit	8	1	9
Special Blue Cross/Blue Shield deduction	8	0	8
Excess of percentage over cost depletion, fuels	7	0	7
Other business preferences*	27	28	55
Total	576	88	664
Accelerated depreciation/expensing provisions	356	306	662
Total Revenue from Business Preferences	932	394	1,326

*None on the special business tax provisions in this category exceed $5 billion over the 10 year budget window. Source: U.S. Department of the Treasury, Office of Tax Analysis.

---

businesses such as partnerships, S corporations, and sole proprietorships. The estimate for the repeal of the R&E tax credit assumes that it is a permanent provision in the baseline.

[63] Repeal of other tax provisions, such as last-in first-out (LIFO) method and the cash method of accounting, also would potentially broaden the tax base. However, those changes have not been considered here for several reasons. Repeal of the LIFO method would include inflationary gains in the value of inventories in the tax base, which is inconsistent with proper income measurement and, more importantly, would disadvantage investment in inventories relative to other forms of investment. Repeal of cash accounting would significantly increase compliance costs, particularly for small businesses. A more detailed discussion of simplified accounting for small businesses is contained in Chapter IV

Although they distort certain investment decisions, a number of the provisions listed in table 3.1 are likely to reduce the tax burden on new investments. These include the deduction for U.S. production/manufacturing, the R&E credit, and accelerated depreciation/expensing.[64] Together, these three provisions account for about 80 percent of the revenue gain from business base broadening. Accelerated depreciation alone accounts for about 50 percent of the revenue gain. As mentioned in the introduction to this chapter, repealing these provisions reduces the incentive to undertake new investments. This reduced incentive to invest can hurt labor productivity, which is central to higher living standards for workers in the long run.

Thus, in evaluating the base broadening illustrated by table 3.1, it is important to recognize that the repeal of several provisions would discourage investment and have a detrimental effect on economic growth. Indeed, the Treasury Department estimates that the combined policy of base broadening and lowering the business tax rate to 28 percent might well have little or no effect on the level of real output in the long run because the economic gain from the lower corporate tax rate may well be largely offset by the economic cost of eliminating accelerated depreciation.

If instead the accelerated depreciation provisions were retained, the revenue gained from base broadening would fall to roughly $650 billion over 10 years, and would allow the federal business tax rate to be lowered only to 31 percent. While the reduction in the business tax rate would be more limited, the Treasury Department estimates that this approach would contribute somewhat more substantially to the growth of the economy with the level of real output in the long run rising by about 0.5 percent.

These estimates, however, do not completely account for the economic benefits of rate reduction. The economic benefits are measured as the change in national output in a model[65] that accounts for the changes in the incentives to save and invest in the United States in general and also changes in incentives to invest in the corporate sector or, instead, in a non-corporate sector that includes businesses and owner-occupied housing. However, these estimates do not account for the economic benefits that would result from lowering the distortion between debt and equity financing that comes from a lower business tax rate or from smaller inter-asset distortions (e.g., between equipment and structures) that would result from base broadening or a lower business tax rate. In addition, these

---

[64] This includes repeal of provisions that allow the immediate write-off of an investment's costs (i.e., section 179, which currently allows limited expensing for small businesses).

estimates assume that the base-broadening measures, other than repealing accelerated depreciation, do not affect marginal investment decisions.

While the Treasury Department's model allows for taxes to influence capital flows into and out of the United States, the assumed effect is relatively modest. To some extent, the reduction in business tax rates under the revenue-neutral approaches discussed here is not large. For example, lowering the business tax rate to 31 percent in 2008 would mean that instead of having the second highest statutory corporate tax rate among the 30 OECD countries, the United States would have the third highest tax rate, while with a 28-percent U.S. statutory corporate tax rate, the United States would have the fifth highest tax rate. The estimated effects for larger changes (e.g., a 20-percent corporate tax rate) may well be considerably more substantial than would be suggested by the Treasury Department model and may be necessary to make the United States more competitive.[66]

Instead of lowering the tax rate, the revenue from base broadening could be used to allow partial expensing of tangible capital beyond the limited accelerated depreciation and expensing currently permitted.[67] The Treasury Department estimates that base broadening (including repeal of accelerated depreciation) would raise sufficient revenue ($1.3 trillion over 10 years) to allow partial expensing of 35 percent of business investment.[68] Partial expensing is

---

[65] The same model is used to estimate the economic benefits of the other tax changes discussed in this report.

[66] Effects on capital inflows would also need to consider the possibility that other countries might lower their corporate tax rates in response to a reduction in the U.S. business income tax rate. If other countries responded to a U.S. rate reduction by reducing their tax rates, capital inflows might be more modest and the economic benefits of the rate reduction might be dampened.

[67] It is sometimes noted that if considerably faster write-off of investment were allowed, the deductibility of interest (and the inclusion of interest income in the business tax base) would also need to be reconsidered. The concern is that tangible investment that is debt-financed, where the interest expense would be deductible, might face a substantial negative effective marginal tax rate. Of course, the effective marginal tax rate would also depend on the tax treatment of debt holders. The degree of partial expensing contemplated for this approach (i.e., 35 percent) is likely not large enough to warrant a substantial change to the tax treatment of interest, which would raise other issues, such as the appropriate tax treatment of financial services. Note that in the discussion of a BAT approach in Chapter II, which would provide full expensing, interest would be completely removed from the tax base. A more detailed discussion of the tax treatment of interest is provided in the section, "Tax bias that favors debt financing," in Chapter IV.

[68] For depreciable assets, this approach would allow for 35 percent of new investment to be expensed and 65 percent to be recovered based on economic depreciation. Existing stocks of equipment and structures would be depreciated as under current law. Partial expensing also would be extended to purchases of inventories, but without transition relief. Extending the benefits of partial expensing to inventories helps to promote uniformity in the taxation of the

likely to do more than lowering the business tax rate to increase real output because partial expensing targets the tax benefits to new investment, while a reduction in the tax rate benefits the return from new investment and existing assets alike. Accordingly, the Treasury Department estimates that 35-percent expensing with no reduction of the business tax rate would increase real output in the long run by about 1.5 percent, well above the 0.5 percent increase that is estimated for a revenue- neutral reduction in the business tax rate to 31 percent with the retention of accelerated depreciation.

An important advantage of lowering the business tax rate, relative to expensing, is that a lower rate would reduce the type of tax planning that takes advantage of differences in tax rates among countries. For example, a corporation in a high-tax country may attempt to shift income to an affiliate in a low-tax country. This type of tax planning is economically wasteful. The business incurs a direct cost in hiring expertise to structure such transactions and to avoid or resolve controversies with tax authorities. In addition, and perhaps more importantly, the business may alter its behavior in an inefficient way by structuring its operations and finances to shift income. Also, to the extent that an investment potentially located in the United States is expected to earn supra-normal returns when a foreign company is deciding whether to locate in the United States, then a lower tax rate can be a more effective inducement to locate in the United States than partial expensing.

Lowering the Business Tax Rate on the Non-Corporate Sector

As described above, base broadening and lowering the business tax rate would reduce the tax rate applied to business income in all sectors, not just the corporate sector. The non-corporate sector, consisting of flow-through businesses such as partnerships, S corporations, and sole proprietors, where owners pay tax on business profits, plays an important role in the U.S. economy. This sector is a critical source of innovation and risk-taking. Moreover, roughly 30 percent of all business taxes are paid by flow-through businesses through the individual income tax.[69]

Under the approach of base broadening coupled with a lower business tax rate, the lower tax rate would be applied to flow-through businesses by creating a special

---

income earned by alternative investments, thereby encouraging efficient investment decisions that are guided by economic fundamentals rather than by tax considerations.

[69] U.S. Department of the Treasury (2007).

reduced business tax rate as part of the individual income tax. This reduced rate would equal the corporate rate of 28 percent or 31 percent depending on whether accelerated depreciation is retained.[70]

Keeping the corporate and non-corporate tax rates equal mirrors current law, where the top tax rates in the corporate and individual income taxes are 35 percent. Equality of the top rates helps to prevent certain types of tax avoidance. Nevertheless, equality of the top rates does not ensure that corporate and non-corporate business incomes are taxed at the same overall rate. Corporate income would still remain subject to a double tax on equity-financed investments because income earned in the corporate sector would first be taxed under the corporate income tax and then be taxed again when distributed to shareholders as dividends or realized as capital gains. If tax rates for individuals are higher than for businesses, individual taxpayers in the top individual income tax brackets would have an incentive to receive their earnings as profits from flow-through businesses, rather than as wages from corporations, in order to face the top rate on business income of 28 percent or 31 percent instead of the top individual rate of 35 percent.

Transition Issues

One concern with the transition from the present system of business taxation to a new tax system that has a broad base and lower business tax rates is the potential onetime windfall loss that might be imposed on the owners of existing capital assets. For example, the reform approaches discussed in this chapter would disallow in whole or in part unused business tax credits carried over from the years prior to the enactment of the reform. The loss of these prepaid tax assets would reduce the value of the firms with such assets.[71] Although the reform approach would continue to allow deductions for carryforwards of pre-enactment net operating losses, those deductions would be worth less if business tax rates were reduced.[72]

Other factors would mitigate the fall in the value of existing assets and businesses if base broadening were used to fund a reduction in the tax rate. Repealing business tax credits and repealing accelerated depreciation on new

---

[70] Administratively, the lower rate for income received by owners of flow-through businesses would operate similar to the lower tax rates currently in place for dividends and capital gains.

[71] Pearlman (1996).

[72] Carryover tax credits, if retained, would have the same value before and after reform because $1 of tax credit would reduce taxes by $1 either way.

investment would raise the value of existing assets. Under current law, old capital has a lower value than the equivalent amount of new capital because existing assets already have received their tax credits and deductions, and are thus worth less than new assets that are entitled to new credits and accelerated deductions. Repealing accelerated depreciation and credits would eliminate the relative advantage enjoyed by new over old assets and thereby raise the value of existing (old) assets.

Reducing the business income tax rate would raise asset values by reducing deferred tax liabilities, such as those resulting from accelerated depreciation and the deferral of taxes on unrealized capital gains. A reduction in the business tax rate also would reduce deferred tax liabilities generated by unrepatriated foreign source income. The lower tax rate could increase the value of firms that earn substantial income from pure profits or economic returns. In addition, lowering the business tax rate would raise (at least temporarily) the after-tax return earned on existing investments, thereby offering a benefit that offsets any decline in asset values.

Base broadening could instead be used to provide partial expensing for the purchase of new business investments rather than to lower the tax rate. Replacing the existing capital cost recovery system with partial expensing raises some additional valuation effects.

For many assets, reforming the existing cost recovery system in favor of a system that combines 35-percent partial expensing with economic depreciation would lead to a reduction in the marginal effective tax rate. This reduction would occur because the combination of 35-percent expensing and economic depreciation would allow more accelerated tax deductions than those generally offered by the existing tax depreciation system. More accelerated depreciation allowances, while lowering the marginal effective tax rate, also would lower the value of existing assets because existing capital would not benefit from the accelerated depreciation deductions and would compete with new assets that do benefit (i.e., whose after-tax price is lowered by the accelerated deduction). In many cases, however, the fall in asset values would be modest because depreciation allowances on new investments would be only modestly accelerated and because the reform approach described here would permit business to continue to depreciate existing assets, essentially providing substantial transition relief.[73]

Thus, the approaches for reform discussed in this chapter have effects that both increase and decrease firm values. The net effect on the value of any particular

---

[73] In addition, churning of assets – sales made in order to take advantage of more accelerated depreciation deductions – could offset to some degree the decline in value for certain investments.

firm would vary, depending upon the specific tax characteristics of the firm as well as on the specifics of the approach. Nevertheless, if additional transition relief is provided with a view toward avoiding large reductions in asset values, that relief would increase the cost of the approach, which would reduce the benefits if pursued on a revenue-neutral basis.

Distributional Effects

As with the distributional analysis of the BAT discussed in Chapter II, two sets of distributional analyses were produced for the approach outlined above. In the first set, the traditional assumption employed by the Treasury Department – that the corporate income tax is borne by owners of capital – is used. In the second set, the Treasury Department prepared tables assuming that labor bears 70 percent of the corporate income tax. These distribution tables are intended to reflect the differing views on the incidence of the corporate income tax and to build on the increasingly common view that a substantial portion of the corporate income tax is borne by labor.

The analysis indicates, however, that the underlying burden assumptions make little difference in judging the distributional effects of these approaches. The basic conclusion drawn from table 3.2 is that neither of these approaches for reform – either business tax rate reduction nor partial expensing coupled with base broadening – materially affects the distribution of the tax burden. This in part reflects the small size of the tax changes contemplated under these policies, relative to the total tax collected by the U.S. government. In addition, over the budget period, these approaches are revenue neutral on capital income and thus simultaneously raise some taxes and lower others. To the extent that all taxes on capital income are similarly distributed across income classes, it is no surprise that these policy changes would have little effect on the distribution of the tax burden.

The two alternative assumptions of the incidence of the corporate income tax do suggest that the federal tax system would be somewhat less progressive if the corporate income tax is borne primarily by labor. The top 20 percent of families ranked by income would pay 69.6 percent of total federal taxes rather than 71.5 percent if the corporate income tax is assumed to be borne primarily by labor.

Table 3.2. Distribution of the Federal Tax Burden Under Two Assumptions of the Incidence of the Corporate Income Tax

Income Percentile	Corporate Income Tax Borne by Owners of Capital			Labor Bears 70% of the Corporate Income Tax		
	Income Percentile			Labor Bears 70% of the Corporate Income Tax		
		Base Broadening			Base Broadening	
	Administration's Policy Baseline*	Top 28% Business Tax Rate	35% Expensing	Administration's Policy Baseline*	Top 28% Business Tax Rate	35% Expensing
Percent of Federal Taxes Paid						
First Quintile	0.3	0.3	0.3	0.4	0.4	0.4
Second Quintile	2.1	2.2	2.1	2.5	2.5	2.6
Third Quintile	8.0	8.0	8.0	8.7	8.7	8.8
Fourth Quintile	17.9	17.9	17.9	18.7	18.7	18.8
Fifth Quintile	71.5	71.4	71.6	69.6	69.4	69.4
Bottom 50%	5.5	5.6	5.5	6.3	6.4	6.4
Top 10%	54.9	54.8	55.1	52.2	52.1	52.0
Top 5%	42.0	41.9	42.2	38.9	38.8	38.6
Top 1%	23.4	23.3	23.7	20.5	20.5	20.3

Note: Estimates of 2015 law at 2007 cash income levels. Quintiles begin at cash income of: Second $13,310; Third $28,507; Fourth $50,448; Highest $87,758; Top 10% $128,676; Top 5% $177,816; Top 1% $432,275; Bottom 50% below $38,255.

*The Administration's policy baseline is similar to current law but assumes permanent extension of the 2001 and 2003 tax relief.

Source: U.S. Department of the Treasury, Office of Tax Analysis.

C. Territorial Tax Systems

The increased globalization of U.S. businesses and the decline in corporate tax rates abroad have focused attention on the U.S. corporate tax in an international context. Under current U.S. law, U.S. corporations are taxed on their worldwide income, with a limited tax credit for income taxes paid to foreign governments (see Box 3.1 for a more detailed discussion of the U.S. system for taxing international income). However, many U.S. trading partners currently use a "territorial" system, which exempts some or all of the overseas earnings of their businesses from taxation in the home country.

The U.S. system was developed at a time when the United States was the primary source of capital investment and dominated world markets. The global landscape has shifted considerably over the past several decades, with other countries challenging the U.S. position of economic preeminence. The United States is now a net recipient of foreign investment rather than the largest source.

This section considers the possibility of moving to a more territorial system under which active income that is derived from economic activity outside the United States would not be subject to U.S. corporate income tax. Similar to the practice of two-thirds of OECD countries, a company's active foreign income earned abroad would be excluded from the U.S. tax base, thus placing U.S. businesses operating abroad on a more even playing field relative to their foreign competitors.

Underlying this approach is the notion that U.S. multinational corporations provide important benefits to the U.S. economy by creating jobs and higher real wages for workers in the United States. Workers employed by firms that export earn 15 percent more than the average worker in the U.S. economy.[74] Moreover, when a company expands overseas, jobs are created in the United States to support and manage the company's foreign operations. Between 1991 and 2001, U.S. multinational enterprises increased employment in their domestic parents by 5.5 million, nearly twice as much as they increased employment in their foreign affiliates.[75] Moreover, the current U.S. tax system provides a tax disincentive to the repatriation of foreign earnings, which may cause U.S. multinational corporations to forgo U.S. investment.

---

[74] Slaughter (2004).
[75] *Id.*

> **Box 3.1: The U.S. System for Taxing International Income**
>
> Under current law, corporations formed in the United States are subject to tax on their worldwide income, meaning that they are subject to immediate U.S. tax on all of their direct earnings, whether earned in the United States or abroad. However, U.S. corporations with foreign subsidiaries generally are not taxed on the foreign subsidiaries' active business income (such as from manufacturing operations) until the income is repatriated. That is, until that active business income is returned to the United States, typically through a dividend to the parent corporation, U.S. tax is deferred. Not all foreign subsidiary income is subject to deferral, however. For example, U.S. tax is not deferred on passive or easily moveable income of foreign subsidiaries of U.S. corporations, under the so-called "subpart F" anti-deferral rules.
>
> To prevent double taxation of income by both a foreign country and the United States, a U.S. corporation is allowed a foreign tax credit for foreign taxes paid by it and by its foreign subsidiaries on earnings the foreign subsidiaries repatriate. The foreign tax credit is claimed by a taxpayer on its U.S. tax return, and reduces U.S. tax liability on foreign source income.
>
> The foreign tax credit rules are complicated and include several significant limitations. In particular, the foreign tax credit is applied separately to different categories of income (generally distinguishing between "active" and "passive" income). The total amount of foreign taxes within each category that can be credited against U.S. income tax cannot exceed the amount of U.S. income tax that is due on that category of net foreign income after deductions. In calculating the foreign tax credit limitation, the U.S. parent's expenses (such as interest) are allocated to each category of income to determine the net foreign income on which the credit can be claimed. The allocation of expenses to foreign income can increase U.S. tax by reducing the amount of foreign tax that can be credited that year.
>
> This foreign tax credit limitation, however, does allow active income subject to high foreign taxes (usually active earnings of foreign subsidiaries distributed to U.S. parent corporations as dividends) to be mixed with active income subject to low foreign taxes (usually royalties or interest). Thus, if earnings repatriated by a foreign subsidiary have been taxed by the foreign country in excess of the U.S. rate, the resulting "excess" foreign tax (i.e., the amount of foreign tax on the earnings that exceeds the U.S. tax that would be owed on the dividend) may be used to offset U.S. tax on other, lower-taxed foreign source income in the appropriate category. This method of using foreign tax credits arising from high-taxed foreign source income to offset U.S. tax on low-taxed foreign source income is known as "cross crediting."

Worldwide Tax Systems

Although often described as a "worldwide" tax system, the U.S. system for taxing foreign source corporate income is more accurately described as a hybrid between a "pure" worldwide system for taxing foreign source income and a so-called "territorial" system. Under a pure worldwide system, all foreign earnings would be subject to tax by the home country as they are earned, even if earned by a foreign subsidiary. To prevent double taxation, a foreign tax credit could be allowed for all income taxes paid to foreign governments. Under a "pure" territorial system, on the other hand, only income earned at home would be subject to home-country tax.

Efficiency, competitiveness, considerations of fairness and administrability, and revenue concerns all influence international tax policy making and are sometimes in conflict. As a result, no country has a pure worldwide or pure territorial system. Various standards have been proposed to guide the formulation of international tax policy, as discussed in Box 3.2. None of the proposed standards, however, fits all cases and the tax system cannot feasibly be calibrated to have different rules for every conceivable case.

Accordingly, countries with predominantly worldwide systems do not subject all foreign source income earned by foreign subsidiaries of multinational corporations to immediate home-country taxation, largely so that home-based companies are not at a disadvantage in investing in countries with lower tax rates. Moreover, such countries do not provide an unlimited foreign tax credit, because doing so could reduce, or even eliminate, taxes on domestic source income.

Although a predominantly worldwide approach to the taxation of cross-border income was once more prevalent, it is now used by fewer than half of the OECD countries. Instead, many of these countries now use predominantly territorial tax systems that exempt all or a portion of foreign earnings of foreign subsidiaries from home-country taxation. However, to prevent tax avoidance and to maintain government revenues, countries with predominantly territorial systems typically do not exempt certain foreign earnings of foreign subsidiaries, including earnings generated from holding mobile financial assets, or certain payments that are deductible in the jurisdiction from which the payment is made, such as foreign source royalty payments. In both predominantly worldwide and predominantly territorial systems, the rules that determine which types of foreign income are taxed, when the income is taxed, and what foreign tax credits are available to reduce that tax, are complex and can be the source of a great deal of tax planning.

> Box 3.2: Alternative Criteria for Evaluating the Worldwide Allocation of Capital[76]
>
> Several standards have been proposed as guides to international tax policy, such as capital export neutrality, capital import neutrality, and capital ownership neutrality. Under the principle of capital export neutrality, foreign income should be taxed at the home-country tax rate so as not to distort a corporation's choice between investing at home or abroad.[77] Under the principle of capital import neutrality, foreign income should be taxed only at the local rate so that U.S. corporations can compete with their foreign rivals.[78] Under the principle of capital ownership neutrality, the tax system should not distort ownership patterns.[79] Each of these criteria focuses on only a portion of the decision margins facing corporations making cross-border investments. For example, each criterion focuses on investment in tangible capital without considering the critical role of the location of intangible capital.
>
> Capital export neutrality and capital import neutrality make assumptions for which there is very little empirical evidence. One assumption relates to the supply of capital available to U.S. multinational corporations. For example, capital export neutrality assumes that all investment by U.S. corporations comes from domestic saving – more specifically from a fixed pool of capital available to the U.S. corporate sector. Capital import neutrality and capital ownership neutrality assume that capital is supplied at a fixed rate by the integrated world capital market. All of these standards ignore the presence of intangible assets and how they affect the relationship between investments in different locations, or how opportunities for income shifting under alternative tax systems alter effective tax rates in different locations.

---

[76] U.S. Department of the Treasury (2007). See also Grubert and Altshuler (forthcoming).

[77] Musgrave (1963).

[78] Musgrave (1963).

[79] Capital ownership neutrality has been proposed by Desai and Hines (2003). These standards (capital export neutrality, capital import neutrality, and capital ownership neutrality) assume worldwide efficiency as the goal. Another standard, national neutrality, assumes that home governments cannot obtain reciprocal concessions necessary to approximate worldwide efficiency.

> Therefore, even if the assumption that an integrated worldwide capital market offers financing to corporations on the same terms regardless of where they are based is accepted, that alone is not a sufficient basis for choosing the optimal policy. Consider a potential investment in a low-tax location. The question is - with what other investments in that or other locations does it compete? Various situations are possible. One example might be a locational intangible, like a fast-food trademark that requires that the corporation produce locally in order to supply its customers. In that case, all competitors compete in the same location and should bear the same (presumably local) tax burden. Another example is a mobile intangible, like the design of a computer chip that can be produced in various locations for the worldwide market. In that case, the competitors for the potential low-tax investment may be in high-tax locations including the United States. Capital import neutrality and capital ownership neutrality implicitly assume the first case, such as where capital ownership fits the case of various bidders for an existing asset with a given product and a circumscribed local market that will not be altered by the transaction. By contrast, capital export neutrality leans toward the second case, where all affiliate production substitutes for domestic U.S. production. None of the proposed standards fits all cases and tax policy cannot feasibly be calibrated to have different rules for different cases.

Under the current U.S. system, taxpayers may be able to set up their operations either to avoid the deemed repatriation of foreign profits under anti-deferral rules, or to minimize, through the use of the foreign tax credits, U.S. tax on foreign profits actually repatriated to the United States. These approaches effectively can allow a corporation to engage in "self-help territoriality." For example, creditable foreign taxes associated with dividends paid from high-taxed foreign profits may shield foreign source royalties from U.S. tax, while low-taxed foreign profits may be left abroad, thereby deferring U.S. taxation on those low-taxed profits indefinitely. Depending on the type of predominantly territorial system chosen, current U.S. law may be more favorable to many U.S. corporate taxpayers than a predominantly territorial system.

In part because of self-help territoriality, the current U.S. system for taxing cross- border corporate income raises little revenue from the taxation of dividends. U.S. tax on all corporate foreign income was about $18.4 billion in 2004, the most recent year for which data are available. Importantly, a relatively small part of that revenue, at most 20 percent, was derived from dividends paid by foreign subsidiaries to their U.S. parents. Foreign source royalties, as well as foreign source interest and income from foreign subsidiaries not eligible for deferral under the current system, represent a much more substantial source of tax revenue than dividends.

In addition to raising little revenue, the present system also leads to distortions in economic behavior. For example, to avoid the residual U.S. tax on repatriated earnings, U.S. corporations may choose not to repatriate foreign earnings and thereby forgo U.S. investment opportunities. In addition, U.S. corporations engage in complex planning and incur significant planning costs to reduce the residual tax on repatriations.[80]

Territorial Tax Systems

More than half of OECD countries use a type of territorial system that exempts dividends from abroad from home-country tax. These systems, generally referred to as "dividend exemption" systems, have been proposed previously in the United States and could reduce some of the economic distortions imposed by the current U.S. tax system.

Although the details of a dividend exemption system can vary greatly, a "basic" dividend exemption system, discussed in greater detail in the next section, is likely to increase U.S. corporate income tax revenues. At the present 35-percent statutory corporate tax rate, the Treasury Department estimates that the revenue increase would be substantial, roughly $40 billion over a 10-year period. This revenue gain arises primarily from the elimination of foreign tax credits that, in effect, shield a considerable portion of low-taxed non-dividend foreign source income, such as certain royalties, from U.S. tax.[81] In other words, because the basic dividend exemption system does not exempt many types of foreign source income and because the foreign tax credit otherwise arising from exempt dividends would be eliminated, low-taxed, non-exempt foreign income would be subject to U.S. tax with a much smaller available foreign tax credit, which would result in a large tax increase. In addition, the allocation of expenses to exempt foreign source income increases U.S. tax because such expenses are effectively disallowed.

---

[80] See, for example, the transactions addressed in IRS Notices 2006-85 and 2007-48, involving foreign subsidiary purchases of U.S. parent stock intended to repatriate funds to the United States without U.S. tax. Also, see the discussion in Altshuler and Grubert (2003) and Desai and Hines (2003).

[81] Currently, foreign source royalties are commonly shielded from U.S. taxation by the taxpayer's cross-crediting between high-taxed dividends and low-taxed royalties.

One way to address the expected tax increase that would result from adopting a basic dividend exemption system would be to extend the exemption beyond foreign subsidiary dividends to include certain foreign source royalties. However, either a full or partial exemption for royalties might be viewed as providing a U.S. tax exemption for income that may have arisen from U.S. activities, such as U.S. research and development. Moreover, exempting royalties might lead to a double benefit with respect to this income, as the United States would be providing an exemption for payments that in most foreign jurisdictions would give rise to a deduction. On the other hand, moving to a dividend exemption system without providing some relief for royalties could exacerbate current issues with respect to the migration of a corporation's intangible assets and could also lead to the transfer of research and development activities outside the United States.

In any case, a dividend exemption system would reduce some of the complexity related to the current foreign tax credit regime, primarily because dividends would no longer give rise to foreign tax credits. Other complex provisions would need to remain, including those related to non-exempt income, such as foreign source royalties (assuming foreign source royalties remain subject to U.S. tax) and interest, as well as income inclusions resulting under the subpart F rules. Moreover, rules regarding the pricing of transactions between U.S. corporations and their foreign affiliates (the so-called "transfer pricing" rules) would come under increased pressure, as the move to a basic territorial system would increase the incentive to shift income and assets to low-taxed offshore jurisdictions. However, extending the exemption system to include additional forms of business income, such as royalties, could relieve some of that pressure and in addition allow for further simplification.

Types of Territorial Approaches

Basic Dividend Exemption System

As noted above, more than half of the members of the OECD employ a dividend exemption system. Many U.S. territorial tax proposals to date, including those of the Joint Committee on Taxation and the President's Advisory Panel on Federal Tax Reform, are of a dividend exemption variety. Unlike many foreign dividend exemption systems, however, U.S. territorial proposals to date have generally required the allocation to (and therefore the disallowance of) a significant amount of expenses to exempt foreign income. A system along the lines of these prior U.S. proposals is referred to here as a "basic" dividend exemption system. Several of the major features of a basic dividend exemption system are discussed below.

Treatment of Active Business Income

Under a basic dividend exemption system, dividends paid by foreign subsidiaries of U.S. corporations would not be subject to U.S. tax, nor would foreign active business income earned directly by foreign branches of U.S. corporations. Gains from the sale of assets that generate exempt income, and gains from sales of foreign corporation shares generating exempt dividends, would also not be subject to tax while losses from the sale of such assets or stock would likewise be disallowed. Non-dividend payments from foreign subsidiaries to U.S. corporations, such as royalties and interest, would remain subject to U.S. tax. Businesses would not receive foreign tax credits for foreign taxes paid (including both subsidiary-level taxes and dividend withholding taxes) that are attributable to earnings repatriated as dividends (or attributable to foreign active business income earned through foreign branches) because this income would not be subject to tax in the United States. Under this system, foreign tax credits would continue to be available with respect to foreign taxes paid on nonexempt foreign income, such as royalties and interest.

Treatment of Mobile Income

Under a basic dividend exemption system, passive and easily moveable income – such as subpart F income under the current U.S. tax system (mobile income) – would continue to be subject to U.S. tax, either when earned directly or when earned by foreign subsidiaries (even if not repatriated). Mobile income could include interest, dividends, rents, and royalties arising from passive assets. Under this approach, a foreign tax credit would be available to offset foreign tax paid on mobile income.

Expense Allocation

Because dividends paid by the foreign subsidiary would not be subject to U.S. tax when received by the U.S. corporate parent under a basic dividend exemption system, business expenses incurred by the U.S. parent attributable to those dividends would be disallowed, either in whole or in part, as a deduction against U.S. taxable income. In addition, expenses attributable to exempt foreign active business income earned directly by a foreign branch of a U.S. corporation would be disallowed. In particular, interest expense incurred by a U.S. corporation to earn exempt foreign earnings would be allocated to those earnings and would be nondeductible, as would an appropriate portion of general and administrative expenses. Because royalties would continue to be subject to U.S. tax, research and experimentation expenses could continue to be fully deductible. To achieve the proper allocation of expenses to taxable income, detailed expense allocation rules, similar to the current expense allocation rules, would be necessary and would inevitably introduce complexity to the system.

If expenses associated with foreign exempt income were disallowed as deductions, a dividend exemption system would create additional incentives for tax planning by multinational corporations to reduce the amount of expenses allocable to foreign income. Again, these pressures also exist under current law because expense allocations to foreign source income can restrict use of foreign tax credits. However, expense allocations would have much broader effects under a dividend exemption system because such expense allocations could directly reduce the deductions that could be taken by taxpayers, not solely restrict the use of foreign tax credits.

Instead of disallowing deductions for expenses allocable to exempt foreign source income, some countries, such as France and Italy, exempt less than 100 percent of foreign subsidiary dividends and directly earned foreign active business income. The benefit of adopting this modification to a basic dividend exemption system is that it allows for the elimination of some relatively complex rules associated with expense allocation.

Transfer Pricing

A basic dividend exemption system would also create additional incentives for multinational corporations to use transfer pricing to minimize taxable income generated by domestic operations and maximize income generated by active foreign business operations. These pressures also exist under current law, and a large body of rules has evolved to enforce "arm's length" transfer pricing among related parties. However, the pressures are more pronounced in a basic dividend exemption system because shifting income and assets overseas may result in exempt foreign source income, rather than produce income that is eligible merely for deferral of tax, as under the current U.S. system. To the extent that transfer pricing enforcement cannot withstand the increased pressures, significant abuse concerns might arise.

Revenue Consequences of Basic Dividend Exemption System

As noted above, adoption of a basic dividend exemption system by the United States would likely increase corporate income tax revenues. The Treasury Department estimates the 10-year revenue gain associated with a basic dividend exemption system such as outlined above (with no other changes to the U.S.

international tax rules) to be approximately $40 billion at the present 35-percent statutory corporate tax rate. If the corporate tax rate were 28 percent, the 10- year estimate of the revenue gain would increase to $50 billion.[82]

The increase in corporate income tax revenues from adoption of a basic dividend exemption system is a result of two factors. First, the relatively small revenue loss from eliminating the U.S. tax on dividends is more than offset by the full taxation of royalties and other foreign source income still subject to tax. Approximately two-thirds of foreign source royalty payments are essentially exempt from U.S. tax because of cross-crediting with high-taxed dividends. Under a dividend exemption system, royalties would no longer be shielded from U.S. tax by such cross-crediting. Second, the allocation of expenses to exempt foreign source income increases U.S. tax because that allocation has greater negative consequences under a dividend exemption system (deduction disallowance) than under current law (decreased ability to use foreign tax credits).

Indeed, under a basic dividend exemption system, because of the continued full taxation of royalties and the disallowance of deductions for expenses attributable to exempt foreign income, the *effective* tax rate on investment in a low-tax location would *increase*, not decrease. Grubert and Mutti (2001) estimate that the effective tax rate for a typical investment in a low-tax affiliate would increase from about 5 percent under current law to about 9 percent under a basic dividend exemption.[83] For an investment in intangible assets, the effective tax rate would increase from about 26 percent to 35 percent. These estimates do not take income shifting into account and, thus, may overestimate the actual burdens corporations may face in low-tax countries.

---

[82] Lowering the U.S. corporate tax rate to 28 percent generally would increase the amount of foreign tax credits potentially available from high-taxed dividends to shield, through cross-crediting, foreign source royalties and interest from U.S. tax. Under a basic dividend exemption system, however, taxes on exempt dividends could no longer be used in such cross-crediting. The effective elimination of this additional amount of foreign tax credits, and ensuing loss of cross-crediting, accounts for the increased revenue gain from adopting basic dividend exemption under a lower corporate tax rate.

[83] Based on Commerce Department data, these estimates assume that the investment abroad is comprised of 85 percent tangible assets and 15 percent intangible assets and is financed with a mix of debt (U.S. and local) and equity. The effective tax rate is a weighted average of the rates, derived from the Treasury Department's tax files. The affiliate is assumed to be located in a country with a statutory tax rate of 7 percent, which in turn is assumed to equal the local effective tax rate on net equity. The effective tax rate estimates include the estimated efficiency loss from deferred repatriations based on Grubert and Mutti (2001).

Alternative Territorial Approaches

A basic dividend exemption system might reduce economic distortions by addressing the problem of forgone domestic investment opportunities and eliminating certain tax avoidance costs. However, as discussed above, it would *increase* the overall tax burden on foreign source income of U.S. corporations primarily because of the greater tax on royalty income, which, in many cases, is currently shielded from U.S. tax through cross-crediting, would incur greater U.S. tax, and because the allocation of parent expenses to exempt foreign source income would result in disallowance of certain deductions. This higher level of tax may well affect a variety of business decisions including the location of investment.

The higher tax burden could be addressed by exempting other foreign source income in addition to dividends and active foreign source income earned through foreign branches, or by relaxing the current expense allocation rules. Such a system would potentially allow for additional simplification but, depending on the details of the system, could pose abuse and revenue-loss problems, including the loss of tax revenue generated from what is currently U.S. source income. For example, an approach that also exempts 50 percent of royalties and requires no disallowance of interest and general and administrative expenses would cost $75 billion over a 10-year period.

Alternative territorial approaches include:

Narrower definition of mobile income. Dividend exemption approaches generally assume that mobile income (which would be subject to immediate U.S. tax when earned either by foreign subsidiaries or directly by U.S. corporations) includes more than passive income earned by non-financial institutions. While the details vary, as a general matter, dividend exemption proposals tend to tax currently certain types of foreign active business income deemed to be easily moveable. Expanding the categories of exempt income could allow for simplification and would reduce the revenue gains associated with dividend exemption.

Extension of the exemption to certain foreign source royalties and interest. An alternative territorial approach could exempt, in whole or in part, royalties and interest received by U.S. corporations in the active conduct of a trade or business. Another alternative would be to treat income received by U.S. corporations from foreign subsidiaries in the form of royalties and interest as exempt income on a look-through basis. In other words, if such income were allocable to the active business income of the payor, it would be eligible for exemption.

As discussed above, exempting royalties could be controversial, as some may view it as providing a U.S. tax exemption for income that may have arisen from U.S. activities, such as U.S. research and development. On the other hand, moving to a dividend exemption system without providing some relief for royalties could exacerbate current issues with respect to intangible migration, and lead to the transfer of research and development activities outside the United States.

Reduce expense disallowance. Another alternative territorial system would limit exempt income to foreign source dividends and foreign active business income of foreign branches of U.S. corporations, but relax the rules disallowing a U.S. parent corporation's interest and general and administrative expenses attributable to exempt foreign income. This alternative would disallow only a fixed percentage of appropriately attributable expenses, thereby possibly allowing deductions of expenses attributable to foreign source income against U.S.-source income. Alternatively, all expenses could be fully deductible but only a percentage of foreign source dividends and directly earned foreign active business income would be exempt, similar to what France, Italy, and other countries do (see Box 4.2 for a discussion of dividend taxation by other countries).

If a portion of interest and general and administrative expenses are not allocated to exempt foreign source income (and, therefore, not disallowed), the effective tax rate on investment in low-tax countries could be negative (indicating that the investment has a higher return after taxes than before taxes) because the tax saving from the U.S. deduction could exceed the foreign tax on the income. This result might encourage multinational corporations to shift business activities abroad that otherwise would be conducted in the United States but for tax motives.

In sum, a basic dividend exemption system would remove the tax disincentive to the repatriation of foreign earnings. It would also reduce some of the complexity related to the current system with respect to foreign tax credits, primarily because dividends would no longer give rise to foreign tax credits. Nevertheless, other complex provisions would remain, for example, with respect to non-exempt income, such as foreign source royalties and interest as well as subpart F inclusions. As noted above, the transfer pricing rules may come under increased pressure, as the move to a basic dividend exemption system could increase the incentive to shift income and assets to low-tax offshore jurisdictions. Extending the foreign source income exemption to include other active business income, such as royalties, could allow for additional simplification, would eliminate the revenue raised by moving to a basic dividend exemption system, and could relieve some of the increased pressure on the transfer pricing rules, but could raise other issues and concerns.

REFERENCES

Altshuler, Rosanne and Harry Grubert. 2001. "Where Will They Go if We Go Territorial? Dividend Exemption and the Foreign Location Decisions of U.S. Multinational Corporations." *National Tax Journal* 54(4): 787-809.

Altshuler, Rosanne and Harry Grubert. 2003. "Repatriation Taxes, Repatriation Strategies, and Multinational Financial Policy." *Journal of Public Economics* 87(1): 73-107.

Altshuler, Rosanne, Harry Grubert, and T. Scott Newlon. 2001. "Has U.S. Investment Abroad Become More Sensitive to Tax Rates?" In *International Taxation and Multinational Activity 2001,* ed. James R. Hines, Jr., 9-32. Chicago: University of Chicago Press.

Ault, Hugh J. 2003. "U.S. Exemption/Territorial System vs. Credit-Based System." *Tax Notes International* November 24: 725-729.

Desai, Mihir A. and James R. Hines Jr. 2003. "Evaluating International Tax Reform." *National Tax Journal* 56(3): 487-502.

Desai, Mihir A., C. Fritz Foley, and James R. Hines Jr. 2001. "Repatriation Taxes and Dividend Distortions." *National Tax Journal* 54(4): 829-851.

Gann, Hal and Roy Strowd. 1995. "Perspectives on Guidance: Deferred Tax Accounting For Tax Reform Proposals. *Tax Notes,* July 3, 1995.

Graetz, Michael, and Paul W. Oosterhuis. 2001. "Structuring an Exemption System for Foreign Income of U.S. Corporations." *National Tax Journal* 54(4): 771-786.

Grubert, Harry. 1998. "Taxes and the Division of Foreign Operating Income among Royalties, Interest, Dividends, and Retained Earnings." *Journal of Public Economics* 68(2): 269-290.

Grubert, Harry. 2001. "Enacting Dividend Exemption and Tax Revenue." *National Tax Journal* 54(4): 811-827.

Grubert, Harry and Roseanne Altshuler. Forthcoming. "Corporate Taxes in the World Economy: Reforming the Taxation of Cross-Border Income." In *Fundamental Tax Reform: Issues, Choices and Implications*, eds. John Diamond and George Zodrow. Cambridge: The MIT Press.

Grubert, Harry and John Mutti. 1991. "Taxes, Tariffs and Transfer Pricing in Multinational Corporation Decision Making." *Review of Economics and Statistics* 33: 285-293.

Grubert, Harry and John Mutti. 2001. *Taxing International Business Income: Dividend Exemption versus the Current System*. Washington, DC: American Enterprise Institute.

Hines, James R., Jr. and Eric Rice. 1994. "Fiscal Paradise: Foreign Tax Havens and American Business." *Quarterly Journal of Economics* 109: 149-182.

Joint Committee on Taxation. 2005. *Options to Improve Tax Compliance and Reform Tax Expenditures,* JCS-02-05.

Kleinbard, Edward D. 2007. "Throw Territorial Taxation from the Train." *Tax Notes,* February 5: 547-564.

Lyon, Andrew B. and Peter R. Merrill. 2001. "Asset Price Effects of Fundamental Tax Reform." In *Transition Costs of Fundamental Tax Reform, eds.* Kevin A. Hassett and R. Glenn Hubbard, 58-92. Washington, DC: AEI Press.

Musgrave, Peggy B. 1963. *Taxation of Foreign Investment Income: An Economic Analysis*. Baltimore, MD: John Hopkins Press.

Pearlman, Ronald A. 1996. "Transition Issues in Moving to a Consumption Tax: A Tax Lawyer's Perspective." In *Economic Effects of Fundamental Tax Reform,* eds. Henry J. Aaron and William G. Gale, 393-427. Washington, DC: The Brookings Institution.

The President's Advisory Panel on Federal Tax Reform. 2005. *Simple, Fair, and Pro-Growth: Proposals to Fix America's Tax System.* Washington, DC: The U.S. Government Printing Office.

Slaughter, Matthew J. 2004. "Globalization and Employment by U.S. Multinationals: A Framework and Facts." Paper presented at the Tax Council Policy Institute Sixth Annual Tax Policy & Practice Symposium, February 10-11, 2005.

Sullivan, Martin A. 1995. *Flat Taxes and Consumption Taxes: A Guide to the Debate.* New York: American Institute of Certified Public Accountants.

U.S. Department of the Treasury. 2007. *Treasury Conference on Business Taxation and Global Competitiveness: Background Paper.* Washington, DC: U.S. Department of the Treasury.

Chapter 4

ADDRESSING STRUCTURAL PROBLEMS WITH THE U.S. BUSINESS TAX SYSTEM

In contrast with the previous chapters, this chapter considers several approaches that address specific areas of business income taxation that could be reformed separately or in the context of broad-based reform. A comprehensive approach, however, is likely to be more effective in improving the competitiveness of the U.S. business tax system than addressing specific issues outside of broad-based business tax reform. These approaches are presented as part of a fully informed public policy discussion.

The first section considers approaches to addressing the issue of tax cascading and multiple taxation of corporate income by changing the tax treatment of corporate capital gains and intercorporate dividends. Other sections consider approaches to address the tax bias that favors debt finance, the tax treatment of certain international income, the tax treatment of losses, book-tax conformity, and other illustrative areas regarding tax administration.

A. MULTIPLE TAXATION OF CORPORATE PROFITS

The current U.S. income tax system generally taxes corporate profits twice: first under the corporate income tax, and then again when profits are received as dividends or capital gains by individual investors. The U.S. corporate income tax can add additional layers of tax when one corporation owns stock in another corporation and is taxed on dividends received from that other corporation or on realized capital gains from selling the shares of stock of that other corporation. Intercorporate dividends receive relief from triple taxation by means of the dividends received deduction (DRD) for dividends received from a domestic corporation and by means of the foreign tax credit for dividends received from a foreign corporation. Nevertheless, the DRD is often less than 100 percent of dividends received and the foreign tax credit applies only in certain cases and may not entirely offset the additional layer of tax. Moreover, no such relief is available for corporate capital gains taxes from the sale of stock of a domestic corporation, although in certain cases the foreign tax credit is available upon the sale of stock of a foreign corporation. Some analyses consider the estate tax to be an additional potential layer of tax on corporate earnings. The additional layers of tax, sometimes referred to as tax cascading, raise the cost of capital and create a tax bias against intercorporate ownership structures.

Under an ideal income tax system, real (inflation-adjusted) corporate income, including capital gains, would be taxed as it accrues and losses would be deductible as they accrue. The double tax on corporate profits and any tax cascading would be eliminated through integration of the individual and corporate tax systems. Corporate income would be taxed at the same rates as income generated in other businesses, including partnerships and sole proprietorships.

In contrast, under the current tax system, capital gains of corporations are taxed only upon realization at rates up to 35 percent, with no allowance for inflation. Net capital losses of a corporation may not be deducted against ordinary income, but may be carried back up to three years or forward up to five years to offset capital gains. In certain cases, corporations can defer capital gains taxes by exchanging property for other property deemed to be like-kind property or engaging in other types of tax-free transactions. In contrast, capital gains realized directly by individuals and through non- corporate businesses are generally subject to a top tax rate of 15 percent.

1. Corporate Capital Gains

The current tax treatment of corporate capital gains, where tax is paid upon the disposition of an asset, discourages the sale of corporate assets. This "lock-in" effect can prevent business assets from being deployed to their best and highest use, thereby resulting in the misallocation of business assets and capital throughout the economy and reducing economic growth. In addition, even though corporate capital gains are nominally taxed at the same tax rate as regular corporate income, corporate capital gains from the sale of stock can result in multiple layers of tax and a heavy total tax burden. Finally, corporate capital gains are taxed much more heavily than capital gains realized in the non-corporate business sector, which encourages business activities that involve substantial capital gains to be conducted primarily in the non-corporate sector.

Lowering the corporate capital gains rate, which would restore tax treatment available prior to the Tax Reform Act of 1986, would reduce these tax distortions while reducing the overall tax rate on investment.[84] Moreover, a lower corporate capital gains tax rate would be more in line with the tax treatment of corporate capital gains among the United States' major trading partners. For example, most G-7 countries provide an exclusion for sales of corporate holdings of stock that is comparable to the DRD in the United States. This exclusion limits the cascading of taxes.

Current Capital Gains Rules Create Economic Distortions

The current tax treatment of corporate capital gains distorts a number of business decisions in important ways.

Misallocation of Corporate Capital due to Lock-in Effects

Absent tax and competition considerations, corporations would sell assets when another firm could earn a higher rate of return on those assets. Because capital gains tax would have to be paid on realized capital gains, however, a potential buyer would have to expect to earn a sufficiently high rate of return to compensate the selling firm for its capital gains tax. Thus, many appreciated corporate assets may remain with their current owners even though other owners could make more productive use of those assets, resulting in inefficient use of economic resources.[85]

Misallocation of Resources between Corporate and Non-Corporate Sectors

Corporate income is generally taxed at both the corporate and individual levels, resulting in double taxation. Cascading of tax can result when corporations owning stock in other corporations receive dividends or recognize

---

[84] Prior to the Tax Reform Act of 1986, corporate capital gains were taxed at a 28-percent rate while the top rate on regular corporate income was 46 percent.

[85] This distortion, sometimes called the "lock-in" effect, arises as a result of taxing capital gains when realized rather than as they accrue. Attempting to tax capital gains as they accrue, however, would create significant valuation issues with respect to valuing property such as specialized equipment and intangibles and could create cash flow problems for businesses by requiring them to pay tax when no income has been realized.

capital gains from the sale of that stock.[86] In contrast, business income from partnerships and other pass-through entities is subject only to a single layer of tax at the owner level.

The higher taxes on corporate capital gains discourage investment in the corporate sector resulting in the misallocation of capital between the corporate and non-corporate sectors. This shifting is particularly important for real estate and other economic sectors, where the periodic sale of assets is more common. This shifting is economically inefficient because the U.S. capital stock thereby earns a lower overall rate of return and non-corporate investments do not benefit from the greater access to capital and other advantages of the corporate form.

Bias Against Intercorporate Investments

Intercorporate investments in the stock of other corporations are discouraged by the cascading of taxes on corporate income. Multi-tiered corporate structures may enhance corporate productivity by allowing businesses to create corporate joint ventures or meet state regulatory requirements in certain industries.[87]

International Distortions

Several studies have argued that U.S. firms face higher corporate capital gains taxes than competitor firms in other countries. A recent analysis found that 16 of the 27 European Union (E.U.) countries, including all of the larger economies, provide partial or full exemption for the disposition of shares in other corporations, generally with a requirement of 5 percent or 10 percent ownership of the corporation in which the shares are disposed.[88] While other corporate capital gains in these countries are generally taxed at the ordinary corporate tax rate, a number of E.U. countries have reduced their statutory corporate tax rates in recent years. In addition, rollover relief is generally available for corporate restructurings.

---

[86] A triple tax can also arise. If corporation A owns stock in corporation B, the three layers of tax would be: (1) the corporate income tax on the earnings of corporation B that increase the value of its shares, (2) the corporate capital gains tax on corporation A if it sells shares of corporation B, and (3) the individual income tax on shareholders of corporation A if they recognize the income of corporation A by receiving dividends or realizing capital gains from selling their shares. Some analyses consider the estate tax as an additional potential layer of tax on corporate earnings.

[87] Morck (2005) attributes the greater prevalence of complex corporate structures and intercorporate holdings of stock in Europe in part to their partial or full exemption of intercorporate income.

[88] Hare (2007).

Distortion of Transactions - Tax Rates on Dividends Versus Capital Gains

The high tax rate on corporate capital gains as compared to dividends, which generally benefit from the DRD, can distort the form of transactions. For example, a corporation may want to sell its stock in a domestic subsidiary, but doing so would result in a 35-percent tax rate on the capital gain. The corporation could convert the potential capital gains income into dividend income by having the subsidiary borrow money and pay a dividend back to the parent corporation.[89] The selling price of the subsidiary and the capital gain would be reduced by the amount of the dividend. The high 35-percent corporate capital gains tax rate, as compared to the much lower effective tax rate on the dividend, creates a substantial tax penalty on transactions that yield capital gains.[90]

Distortion of Transactions – Selling a Subsidiary's Stock or Its Assets

The high corporate capital gains tax rate exacerbates tax planning issues associated with the sale of a domestic subsidiary and can lead to distortions in the form of the sale, the price received, and the identity of the ultimate buyer. If a corporation sells the stock of the subsidiary and an election (if available) is not made to treat the sale as an asset sale for tax purposes, the buyer takes over the selling corporation's basis of the depreciable property and other assets in the subsidiary. If the assets have been fully depreciated and no additional depreciation deductions can be claimed, the price a potential buyer would be willing to pay would reflect the lack of depreciation deductions. If the corporation instead sells the assets of the subsidiary, the basis of assets is stepped up to the market value (assuming that the fair market value is greater than the depreciated tax basis). Some potential buyers would be willing to pay a higher price because they could recover part of the purchase price by re-depreciating the assets like new assets. Thus, the selling corporation must consider the tax

---

[89] Certain waiting period provisions in the tax code, as well as certain judicial doctrines, are intended to limit the ability of corporations to accomplish this type of income conversion.

[90] For example, if the corporation owned less than 20 percent of the stock of a domestic corporation, the DRD would be 70 percent, and the effective tax rate on the dividend would be 10.5 percent as compared to a 35-percent rate on a capital gain. If the corporation owned 20 percent or more, but less than 80 percent of the stock, the DRD would be 80 percent, and the effective tax rate would be 7 percent. If the corporation owned 80 percent or more of the stock, the DRD would be 100 percent and there would be no tax on the dividend. If the stock were stock of a foreign corporation, a DRD would generally not be available for dividends paid on the stock, but a foreign tax credit may be available to reduce tax on the dividend. Gain on the sale of foreign corporate stock could be recharacterized as a dividend pursuant to section 1248, however, and a foreign tax credit may thereby be available.

situations of potential buyers as well as its own tax situation in negotiating the selling price and the form of the sale.[91] High corporate capital gains tax rates increase the consequences of tax-induced distortions of business decisions about how to sell a subsidiary, the price paid, and to whom the subsidiary is sold.

In some cases, corporations have structured transactions to defer or avoid capital gains taxes, resulting in complaints about tax abuses, lost federal revenues, and efforts by Congress and the Treasury Department to eliminate the use of specific types of avoidance transactions.

Transactions can sometimes be structured as non-taxable business reorganizations or, for certain tangible assets, as like-kind exchanges. As a result, stock or asset sales and spin-offs of subsidiaries can trigger capital gains taxes in some cases but not others. Alternatively, corporations can enter into monetizing transactions to defer capital gains taxes while reducing investment risk and possibly raising cash.[92] For example, one study examined cases in which corporations issued securities to hedge an appreciated position, thereby raising cash and deferring capital gains taxation.[93]

Higher Cost of Capital

The corporate capital gains tax raises the cost of capital for corporations. While standard calculations generally ignore corporate capital gains taxes, calculations in one study show that corporate taxes on the sale of assets (including recapture of depreciation as ordinary income) could raise the cost of capital for equipment and software by 0.7 percent, assuming that the assets were sold after 10 years.[94]

Using recent estimates of the responsiveness of investment to the tax-adjusted cost of capital, the study estimated that the current corporate capital gains tax reduces investment in equipment and software by 0.35 percent to 0.70 percent, or $4 billion to $7 billion per year at current levels. The effect on investment in structures is larger because the longer useful life means there is more remaining value that can be sold. Thus, for investment in structures, the corporate capital gains tax raises the cost of capital by 9.3 percent if the investments are expected to be sold after 10 years and 4.5 percent if sold after 20 years.

---

[91] Section 338(h)(10) allows the parties to elect to treat a stock sale as an asset sale in certain situations. Section 33 8(g) also permits the buyer to obtain asset sale treatment, while the seller's stock sale would still be respected for tax purposes and the subsidiary could incur tax on the deemed sale of its assets.

[92] Section 1259 treats certain monetizing transactions as taxable dispositions of the monetized assets.

[93] Gentry and Schizer (2003).

[94] Hassett and Viard (2007).

Significance of Corporate Capital Gains

In 2005, the latest year for which data are available, corporations reported $136 billion in corporate capital gains, representing about 12 percent of total corporate taxable income. Capital gains were a larger percentage of corporate taxable income during the late 1990s, reaching 23.2 percent of taxable income in 2000 (table 4.1).

The main types of assets that generate corporate capital gains are: (1) investment assets such as stocks and bonds, (2) assets (including land) held for long-term investment rather than for ordinary business purposes, (3) self-created patents, (4) goodwill, and (5) real or depreciable assets.[95] Corporate capital gains from the sale of business property, including machinery, equipment, structures, and other property used in the business, accounted for 35 percent of corporate capital gains,[96] with the rest including capital gains from the sale of securities, interests in corporate and non-corporate businesses, and intangible assets such as patents.

The largest amounts of corporate capital gains are in manufacturing (22 percent), services (21 percent), and insurance (11 percent). Capital gains represent the largest shares of taxable income in real estate, agriculture, mining, and insurance. While manufacturing reported the largest dollar amount of corporate capital gains, this represented a lower than average percentage of taxable income.

While about 6 percent of all corporations realized capital gains, 45 percent of corporations with at least $1 billion in assets reported capital gains. The largest

---

[95] All or a portion of gains from the sale of certain types of depreciable property are recharacterized from capital gain to ordinary income in order to recapture prior depreciation deductions that offset ordinary income. Section 1245 generally requires the recapture of the full amount of prior depreciation deductions with respect to personal property and most other tangible property (other than a building) used in a business. Section 1250 generally applies to depreciable real property, and generally only requires the recapture of the excess of the amount of accelerated depreciation deductions over the amount of depreciation determined under the straight-line method. For sales of equipment and business personal property, any gain resulting from previous depreciation deductions is recaptured as ordinary income. Most gains on structures and other real property are taxed as capital gains because there is effectively no recapture for gains on such assets. Recapture would apply to the excess of accelerated deprecation over straight-line depreciation, but residential and non-residential structures are now depreciated using the straight-line method. Section 291(a) currently recaptures 20 percent of the amount of section 1250 gain that would be recaptured if the property were subject to section 1245. This provision tends to eliminate churning incentives for most structures. Buyers of used depreciable property can claim depreciation deductions on the same basis as buyers of new property.

[96] Most of the gains from the sale of business property appears to be capital gains from the sale of machinery, equipment, vehicles, and other tangible property used in manufacturing and other types of businesses.

100 firms (by assets) reporting capital gains accounted for 55 percent of total gains, and firms reporting at least $100 million in assets accounted for two-thirds of the total.

Table 4.1. Capital Gains of Corporations, 1992 – 2005

Year	Number of Corporations	Corporations with Capital Gains	Percent of Corporations with Capital Gains	Corporate Capital Gains	Capital Gains as a Percent of Taxable Income
			(number of returns in thousands, dollar amounts in billions)		
1992	2,077	138	6.6	50.7	13.5
1993	2,056	149	7.3	60.9	14.1
1994	2,311	155	6.7	49.4	10.1
1995	2,312	162	7.0	68.9	12.3
1996	2,317	168	7.3	73.2	11.8
1997	2,247	174	7.7	103.1	15.6
1998	2,249	171	7.6	117.7	18.5
1999	2,198	164	7.5	145.7	21.5
2000	2,172	159	7.3	171.4	23.2
2001	2,136	127	5.9	117.6	18.9
2002	2,099	104	5.0	75.2	13.0
2003	2,047	105	5.1	85.4	12.9
2004	2,027	114	5.6	102.9	12.6
2005	1,975	112	5.7	136.2	11.8

Note: Capital gains of S corporations, regulated investment companies, real estate investment trusts, and personal service corporations are not included.
Source: IRS Statistics of Income, Corporate Income Tax Returns for 1992 through 2005.

Approaches Regarding Corporate Capital Gains[97]

Reduce the Corporate Capital Gains Tax Rate

The distortions created by the current high tax rates on corporate capital gains could be addressed by setting the corporate capital gains rate equal to the maximum tax rate on individual capital gains, currently 15 percent. More limited approaches, such as a 20 percent or 25 percent corporate capital gains rate, would, of course, provide smaller economic benefits.

---

[97] The approaches described in this chapter are not intended to address sales of stock of foreign corporations. Such transactions are addressed by the territorial approach discussed in Chapter III.

A lower corporate capital gains rate would have three principal benefits: (1) reduce the lock-in effect, (2) reduce the uneven treatment of intercompany transactions in the form of dividends versus capital gains, and (3) reduce the uneven taxation of capital gains in the corporate and non-corporate sectors. Moreover, a lower corporate capital gains tax rate would also reduce somewhat the overall tax rate on investment.

As discussed above, the lock-in effect arises in cases where otherwise profitable and economically desirable asset sales are discouraged by the capital gains tax. By discouraging such sales, the lock-in effect prevents assets from flowing to their highest valued uses. Desai and Gentry (2004) found strong lock-in effects on the sale of corporate assets. They found that high corporate capital gains rates reduced the percentages of corporations selling both financial investments and tangible property, reduced the amounts of financial investments and tangible property sold by those corporations that did sell, and reduced the amounts of capital gains realized by corporations.

Using the results of this study, Desai (2006) recently estimated the benefits of reducing lock-in effects by lowering the corporate capital gains rate to 15 percent. Desai estimated that lowering the capital gains rate from 35 percent to 15 percent would permanently increase realized corporate capital gains by 52 percent or $67 billion from an assumed baseline of $128 billion.[98]

The substantial unlocking associated with lowering the corporate capital gains tax rate would reduce the revenue cost of lowering the corporate capital gains tax rate. Indeed, the Desai and Gentry research suggests that the revenue-maximizing rate – the tax rate above which the federal government would actually lose revenue from a higher capital gains tax rate because of the lock-in effect – is probably roughly 25 percent to 26 percent.[99] The Treasury Department estimates that in the absence of any behavioral responses, lowering the corporate capital gains tax rate to 15 percent would cost roughly $220 billion over 10 years, but once the unlocking and other behavioral effects of a lower tax rate are incorporated, the revenue cost of the 15-percent rate would be only roughly $125

---

[98] Desai's simulation uses an elasticity of -0.75 for the long-run increase in capital gains from reductions in the corporate capital gains rate. Using alternative assumptions, Desai estimated long-run increases in realizations between $44 billion and $80 billion. Note that the Desai and Gentry (2004) and Desai (2006) analyses suggest that the response in the first few years of this approach is likely to be considerably larger because the total elasticity, including both short-run and long-run responses, is -1.11.

[99] This estimate is based on Equation 6 in Table 3 of Desai and Gentry (2004), which Desai (2006) cites as the preferred equation. The revenue-maximizing rate in this equation is 25.4 percent, calculated as $0.254 = 1/3.9293$, where 3.9293 is the coefficient on the tax rate variable in the equation.

billion over 10 years. That is, the behavioral responses would offset about 43 percent of the static revenue cost of the lower tax rate.[100]

The second advantage of a lower corporate capital gains tax rate is reduced distortions in business decisions that arise from the differential between the taxation of dividends received by corporations (which typically receive a DRD of 70 percent or more if the payor is a domestic corporation) and capital gains on corporate stock (which are fully taxed in the case of a domestic corporation). A lower corporate capital gains tax rate would reduce tax planning associated with structuring transactions to obtain income in the form of dividends rather than capital gains. A lower corporate capital gains tax rate would also reduce tax-planning efforts to structure transactions to avoid or defer the capital gains tax through like-kind exchanges, monetizing transactions, and tax-free reorganizations.

Desai (2006) estimated that foregone realizations under the current 35-percent capital gains tax rate imposed efficiency costs on the economy of $20.4 billion per year, which is 46 percent of total revenues collected from the corporate capital gains tax.[101] If the corporate capital gains tax rate were reduced to 15 percent, however, the efficiency cost would be reduced to $3.7 billion per year for a gain in economic efficiency of $16.7 billion per year, which is greater than Desai's estimated revenue cost of $15.6 billion per year. That is, the gain in economic efficiency would be about $1.07 per dollar of revenue loss. The high ratio of efficiency gain to tax revenue cost indicates that the capital gains tax is a very distortionary tax. It does not suggest, however, that cutting the tax rate from 35 percent to 15 percent would pay for itself entirely through greater realizations. According to Desai, the lower tax rate would reduce taxes by $15.6 billion.

The third primary advantage of a lower corporate capital gains rate is to reduce the uneven taxation of capital gains between the corporate and non-corporate sectors. Currently, capital gains realized by partnerships, S corporations and sole proprietorships are taxed at a maximum rate of 15 percent under the individual income tax as compared to the 35-percent rate under the corporate tax.[102]

---

[100] In addition to revenue increases from the unlocking effects of a lower tax rate, this estimate also includes other behavioral responses such as conversion of ordinary income into capital gains that may reduce revenues.

[101] While the Desai (2006) calculations are based on a stylized approach to measuring distortions produced by high tax rates, such distortions include inefficiencies associated with productive assets being owned by less efficient businesses, and corporations being prevented from selling assets and stock holdings where the proceeds could be deployed more effectively in higher priority uses.

[102] Under current law, the maximum individual capital gains tax rate is scheduled to increase to 20 percent in 2011.

A lower corporate capital gains tax rate would reduce the tax disadvantage of the corporate form. Currently, the total tax on intercorporate stock holdings is 64.1 percent, compared to 15 percent on individual capital gains from pass-through businesses. Reducing the corporate capital gains rate to 15 percent would reduce the total tax to 53.0 percent.[103]

Reduce Corporate Capital Gains Rates on Intercorporate Stock Gains

A more limited approach to reduce the economic harm associated with the high corporate capital gains rate would be to reduce the tax rate for capital gains from the sale of intercorporate holdings of stock. Such an approach would, in effect, make the taxation of stock gains comparable to the DRD and focus the benefits on limiting tax cascading. Similar to the DRD, the taxation of stock gains could be structured as a percentage exclusion. Exclusions of 50 percent, 60 percent, or 70 percent would result in maximum tax rates of 17.5 percent, 14 percent, and 10.5 percent, respectively. While limiting a lower rate to intercorporate capital gains would reduce the revenue cost, it would leave the capital gains rate on sales of equipment and structures at 35 percent, thereby discouraging such sales.[104]

Reduce the Corporate Tax Rate

The economic distortions created by the high corporate capital gains rate would also be mitigated by lowering the corporate tax rate, as discussed in Chapter III. A separate, lower corporate capital gains tax rate could still be warranted to place capital gains earned in the corporate and non-corporate sectors on a level playing field, although the need for such synchronization from a policy perspective would not be as great depending on the extent to which the corporate tax rate itself were lowered.

---

[103] See also Table 4.3.

[104] When equipment and structures are sold directly, basis is stepped up to fair market value, and this higher amount can be depreciated by the buyer. This step-up in basis partly offsets the higher rate.

Box 4.1: How Corporate Capital Gains Are Taxed in Other Countries

While most G-7 countries typically tax corporate capital gains nominally at the same tax rates as other corporate income, they tend to provide exclusions for corporate capital gains resulting from the sale of corporate stock (table 4.2). Also, the significance of taxing capital gains at the same nominal tax rates is diminished by the lower statutory tax rates generally imposed by other countries. By contrast, Canada provides a 50- percent exclusion that applies to all corporate capital gains.

The intercompany capital gains exclusions provided by most G-7 countries are generally limited to cases in which ownership of the stock holding exceeds some threshold percentage, commonly 5 percent or 10 percent. These provisions are intended to eliminate tax cascading – the multiple layers of tax occurring in transactions among chains of corporations. In addition, certain types of qualifying corporate group restructurings can be achieved on a tax-free basis by rolling over the gain rather than incurring a current tax.

Most, if not all, G-7 countries have a similar exclusion for intercorporate dividends. An important difference is that while most other G-7 countries have exclusions that apply to both intercorporate capital gains and dividends, the United States provides relief from tax cascading only for intercorporate dividends from a domestic corporation, thereby creating a tax bias favoring dividends over capital gains in the case of a domestic corporation. (In the case of dividends from a foreign corporation, a foreign tax credit may be available to reduce tax, and in the case of gain from the sale of foreign corporate stock, some or all of the gain may be treated as a dividend and a foreign tax credit thereby may be available).

Table 4.2. Corporate Capital Gains Taxes in G-7 Countries

Country	Corporate Tax Standard Rate (%)	Corporate Capital Gains Tax Rate (General)	Special Rule for Sale of Corporate Stock	
			Percent Exemption on Gains	Percent Ownership Required
Canada	36.1	50% exempt	No special rule	NA
France	34.4	standard rate	95	5
Germany	38.9	standard rate	95	0
Italy	33.0	standard rate	84	0
Japan	39.5	standard rate	None	NA
United Kingdom	30.0	standard rate	1	10
United States	39.3	standard rate	None	NA

Note: Standard corporate rates include sub-national level taxes. The capital gain exemption percentages on sale of shares in other corporations indicate the percentages of capital gains on corporate shares that are exempt if required participation conditions (minimum control, minimum holding period, industry, etc.) are met. While Canada has no special exemption for sale of corporate stock, the 50-percent exclusion would apply. All countries provide rollover treatment for certain types of corporate reorganizations that are considered non-taxable events.

Source: International Bureau of Fiscal Documentation, PricewaterhouseCoopers LLP.

2. Dividends received deduction

Corporations are generally allowed a DRD on dividends received from holdings of stock in other domestic corporations, but the DRD is incomplete for companies with less than an 80-percent interest. The DRD is 70 percent if a corporation owns less than 20 percent of the stock in another domestic corporation and 80 percent if the corporation owns 20 percent or more, but less than 80 percent of the stock.[105]

The system of partial taxation of intercorporate dividends was introduced into the tax law in 1935 to achieve certain tax policy and non-tax policy goals.[106]

---

[105] In addition to the three basic DRD percentages, a number of special computations apply in certain specific situations. These include intercorporate dividends on debt-financed stock, certain dividends not eligible for a DRD, and a separate deduction for dividends paid on certain preferred stock of public utilities.

[106] Treasury Department testimony to the Senate Finance Committee discussed problems with auditing pyramidal corporate structures and related problems of tax avoidance by shifting income among related companies. Other concerns were the use of leverage and pyramidal structures to allow control of large amounts of assets with little equity and the role that the collapse of such

Previously, all intercorporate dividends were exempt from the corporate income tax. Taxation of 10 percent (and later 15 percent) of intercorporate dividends through a 90-percent DRD was enacted to address concerns about complicated, multi-tiered corporate structures.

A partial DRD leads to tax cascading as corporate income flows through the different levels of corporate ownership. As noted above in the discussion of corporate capital gains, tax cascading discourages investment in the corporate form by raising the cost of capital. A partial DRD may also discourage multi-tiered corporate structures that would otherwise be desirable for business reasons. While dividends received from a foreign corporation are not generally eligible for a DRD, a domestic corporate recipient of the dividend may be able to claim a foreign tax credit that reflects the foreign taxes paid on the repatriated earnings. The foreign tax credit is available only in certain cases, however, and may not entirely offset the additional layer of tax.[107]

Economic Distortions Caused by a Partial Dividends Received Deduction

By failing to allow a full 100-percent deduction for all intercorporate dividends, the tax system can impose multiple layers of tax on intercorporate dividends, which leads to distortions in the allocation of investment by discouraging corporations from investments in other corporations that would be profitable in the absence of the cascading levels of taxes. Under the 70-percent DRD, an additional layer of tax of 10.5 percent is imposed on corporate earnings (30 percent of the 35-percent top corporate tax rate) paid to another corporation as intercompany dividends. Similarly, for an 80-percent DRD, the additional layer of tax is 7 percent. Tax cascading is fully eliminated only for intercorporate dividends within an affiliated group qualifying for the 100-percent DRD.

In addition, a partial DRD and the associated tax cascading may discourage tiered corporate structures that would otherwise be desirable to achieve business purposes such as meeting state or other regulatory requirements. Such potential intercorporate investments may include corporate joint ventures with other firms or venture capital investments in joint ventures with former employees of

---

structures played in the stock market crash of 1929. See Morck (2005), Becht and DeLong (2005), and Mundstock (1988) for discussion of the adoption of partial taxation of intercorporate dividends.

[107] In order to claim a foreign tax credit for foreign corporate income taxes paid on the earnings repatriated, the U.S. corporation must own at least 10 percent of the voting stock of the foreign corporation, and in addition satisfy other limitations.

the firm.[108] A partial DRD may also discourage the free flow of dividends among related companies. This may interfere with the ability of related companies to allocate their limited capital to the most productive investments.

Table 4.3 shows the ultimate effects on individual shareholders of the multiple layers of tax on intercorporate holdings, including the effects of the current 15-percent maximum tax rate on dividends received by individuals and what happens if this provision expires after 2010. With a 70-percent DRD, a corporate tax rate of 35 percent and an individual tax rate of 15 percent on dividends, the total taxes on dividends paid on intercorporate holdings are $50.55 on $100 of earnings in the initial corporation, leaving $49.45 for the corporate shareholder. This is calculated as follows: the first corporation's earnings of $100 are taxed at a 35-percent rate, leaving $65 available for dividends to be paid to the second corporation that owns shares in the first corporation. With a 70-percent DRD, the second corporation pays $6.83 of corporate tax on those dividends (6.83 = 0.35 * (65 - 0.70 * 65)) and pays out the remaining $58.18 to the individual shareholders. Individual shareholders then pay the 15-percent tax on qualified dividends, leaving $49.45 in after-tax income. The after-tax income of the individual shareholders would increase to $51.38 with an 80-percent DRD and to $55.25 with a 100-percent DRD. If the current 15-percent tax rate on dividends expires after 2010 and individuals are taxed at their regular income tax rates, taxes would total $64.86 where there is a 70-percent DRD, and an individual in the top income tax bracket would receive $35.14 in after-tax income.

The example in table 4.3 illustrates that with the 70-percent DRD, the additional layer of tax on intercorporate dividends adds $6.83 tax on $100 of corporate earnings. Increasing the DRD from 70 percent to 100 percent would add $6.83 per $100 of intercorporate dividends to the cash flow of corporations, which would be available for increasing investment. If the 15-percent maximum tax rate on dividends is allowed to expire after 2010, the after-tax income of the shareholder will be reduced by $14.31 (14.31 = 64.86 − 50.55), which leaves less capital for shareholders to reinvest in the economy.

Finally, the cascading of taxes, which results from a partial DRD, can discourage investment by increasing the cost of capital. A rough measure of this effect is provided by the portion of intercorporate dividends subject to tax, which was 6.3 percent of corporate taxable income in 2004 (the most recent data available).

---

[108] Some high-tech and pharmaceutical firms, for example, have formed joint ventures with key scientific and technical employees to provide the employees an opportunity and the capital to pursue certain projects, while offering the parent corporation an opportunity to profit from the venture. Such investments are discouraged by cascading dividend taxes as well as high corporate capital gains tax rates.

Table 4.3. Multiple Layers of Tax on Dividends Paid on Intercorporate Stock Holdings

	15% Individual Tax Rate on Dividends with DRD of:			39.6% Individual Tax Rate on Dividends with DRD of:		
Earnings, Dividends and	70%	80%	100%	70%	80%	100%
1st corporation's earnings	100.00	100.00	100.00	100.00	100.00	100.00
1st corporate tax on	35.00	35.00	35.00	35.00	35.00	35.00
Dividends paid by 1st	65.00	65.00	65.00	65.00	65.00	65.00
Dividends received	-45.50	-52.00	-65.00	-45.50	-52.00	-65.00
2nd corporation's tax on	6.83	4.55	0.00	6.83	4.55	0.00
Dividends paid by 2nd	58.18	60.45	65.00	58.18	60.45	65.00
Shareholder tax on	8.73	9.07	9.75	23.04	23.94	25.74
After-tax dividends to	49.45	51.38	55.25	35.14	36.51	39.26
Total tax - all levels	50.55	48.62	44.75	64.86	63.49	60.74

Source: U.S. Department of the Treasury, Office of Tax Analysis.

Significance of Intercorporate Dividends and Dividends Received Deductions

In 2004, 156,000 corporations, about 8 percent of all C corporations, reported $274 billion of gross intercorporate dividends (table 4.4). About $82 billion of these were eligible for a 100-percent DRD.[109] Another $125 billion of these dividends were eligible for foreign tax credits that would offset U.S. corporate tax to the extent of taxes paid to other countries. Nearly $17 billion in dividends were eligible for the 70-percent or 80-percent DRD, and $9 billion in dividends were eligible for a DRD under other provisions. The total amount of DRDs was $98 billion. After netting out the DRD and the dividends eligible for the foreign tax credit, it appears that about $51 billion in dividends were subject to potentially cascading levels of tax at the corporate level. Intercorporate dividends are highly concentrated among small numbers of firms. In 2004, 75 percent of the total was received by 427 firms with over $10 billion in assets, and 44 percent was received by manufacturing firms.

---

[109] Some intercorporate dividends were netted out in processing the returns. This amount includes an estimate of dividends eligible for the 100 percent DRD but netted out of the reported data. The estimate is based on information reported on Schedules M-1 and M-3.

Table 4.4. Intercorporate Dividends and Dividend Received Deductions, 2004

Dividends Received Variable	Amounts ($B)
Gross dividends	273.7
Dividends eligible for:	
70-percent DRD	12.1
80-percent DRD	4.7
100-percent DRD	82.4
Other DRD	8.9
Foreign tax credit	125.0
Total	233.1
Other dividends, not eligible for DRD or foreign tax credit	40.6
Total DRD	97.7
Dividends subject to tax	51.0
Taxable income	813.9
Number of corporations receiving dividends	156,335
Total number of corporations	2,026,963

Note: The sample does not include S corporations, regulated investment companies, and real estate investment trusts, which are pass-through entities for which the DRD does not apply. Dividends eligible for the 100-percent DRD are estimated partly based on Schedule M-1 and M-3 information because they have been netted out and thus are not shown directly on all returns.

Source: IRS Statistics of Income, Corporate Income Tax File.

Box 4.2: How are Intercorporate Dividends Treated by Other Countries?

G-7 countries have either full or partial exclusions for intercorporate dividends (table 4.5). Morck (2005) provides a list of 30 countries that fully exempted intercorporate dividends as of 1997. However, some of these countries now have some taxation of intercorporate dividends. In the case of E.U. countries this seems to be the result of E.U. directives to eliminate tax rules discriminating in favor of domestic as compared to foreign subsidiaries. In order to limit revenue losses, some countries have adopted modest taxation of both domestic and foreign intercorporate dividends. Some studies have noted that European companies tend to have much more complicated corporate structures with multiple layers of corporate ownership, and attribute this to the previous full exemption of intercorporate dividends.[110]

---

[110] Morck (2005) and La Porta et al. (1999).

Table 4.5. Tax Treatment of Intercorporate Dividends in G-7 Countries

Country	Corporate Tax Standard Rate	Dividends Received Deduction	
		Percent Deduction	Percent Ownership Required
Canada*	36.1	100	0
France*	36.1	95	5
			2 year holding period
Germany*	38.9	95	0
Italy*	33.0	95	0-49.9
		100	50
Japan*	39.5	50	0
United Kingdom*	30.0	100	0
		70	Under 20
United States	39.3	80	20-79.9
		100	80

Note: Standard corporate rates include sub-national level taxes.
*Denotes countries cited in Morck (2005) as having no tax on intercorporate dividends as of 1997.
Source: International Bureau of Fiscal Documentation (2007).

Approaches for Addressing Tax Cascading on Intercorporate Dividends[111]

Increase DRD to 100 Percent

Tax cascading within the corporate sector could be eliminated by increasing the DRD to 100 percent. This would eliminate the current tax bias against intercorporate investments and tiered corporate structures that would otherwise be desirable. A 100 percent DRD would improve the ability of related companies to allocate their limited capital to the most productive investments and for independent firms to undertake joint ventures in corporate form.

An increase in the DRD to 100 percent could encourage retention of otherwise uneconomic investments in the stock of other corporations unless corporate capital gains tax rates are also lowered, as discussed above. Without a change to corporate capital gains rates intercorporate dividends would be tax-free to the

---

[111] The approaches described in this chapter are not intended to address dividends from foreign corporations. The tax treatment of dividends from foreign corporations is addressed in this report by the territorial approach discussed in Chapter III.

owner corporation, but sale of the stock would generally result in capital gains tax at a 35-percent rate.

To the extent that current dividend taxes, both those at the individual level and on intercorporate dividends, have already been capitalized into lower share prices, raising the DRD could provide gains to corporations currently holding stock in other corporations. Of course, any such gains would be subject to corporate capital gains taxes when the stock is sold, assuming no change to the taxation of corporate capital gains. Based on this capitalization effect, some have argued that a 100-percent DRD could distort stock ownership by favoring intercorporate ownership over individual ownership. Because taxation of dividends at the individual level would result in some reduction in the price of a dividend-paying stock, a corporation could purchase the stock at a reduced price reflecting the individual-level tax on dividends, but would not itself be subject to tax on dividends.

Because of concerns about tax avoidance and tax arbitrage schemes involving the ability to deduct interest expense and differential tax treatment of capital gains and dividend income, Congress has periodically enacted and strengthened provisions intended to prevent such schemes given the current DRD structure with partial taxation of intercorporate dividends. It is generally thought to have been largely successful, although there are still periodic controversies and court cases. An increase in the DRD to 100 percent might raise concerns that some previously uneconomic tax-arbitrage schemes would again become profitable so that further anti-abuse provisions would be needed.

Increase and Simplify the Current DRD

As an alternative to increasing the DRD to 100 percent, the current complex system of multiple DRD percentages could be greatly simplified. For example, the 70- percent DRD could be increased to 80 percent and some of the minor categories could also be changed to the same percentage. Overall, this could provide simplification as well as a modest reduction in tax cascading.

B. TAX BIAS THAT FAVORS DEBT FINANCING

The current U.S. tax code favors debt over equity forms of finance because corporations can deduct interest expense, but not the return on equity-financed investment. As noted in the previous section, the return on an equity-financed investment (i.e., corporate profit) is taxed twice, first under the corporate income tax and a second time under the individual income tax as a dividend or capital gain. In contrast, the corporation's ability to deduct interest eliminates the corporate-level tax on the return earned by a debt-financed investment, leaving only the single level of tax paid on interest income under the individual income tax. Even after accounting for the lower tax rates on dividends and capital gains relative to the tax rate on interest income under the individual income tax,[112] and allowing for the ability to defer taxes on capital gains,[113] there remains a strong tax bias in favor of debt over equity financing.[114]

Excessive reliance on debt financing imposes costs on investors because of the associated increased risk of financial distress and bankruptcy. Firms in financial difficulty may be denied sufficient access to credit, suffer key personnel losses, and endure a diversion of management time and energy away from productive activity. Other costs include legal and administrative expenses associated with bankruptcy, uncertainty regarding the ultimate size of those expenses, uncertainty regarding the marketable value of the firm's assets under partial or full liquidation, and risks regarding the ultimate settlement of competing claims on those assets.[115]

Marginal Effective Tax Rates under Debt and Equity Financing

The tax bias in favor of the use of debt over equity financing is reflected in estimates of the marginal effective tax rate for new corporate investment. The marginal effective tax rate is the hypothetical tax rate that, if applied to properly measured income, is equivalent to the tax burden imposed by various features of the tax system. It includes the effects of statutory tax rates at the company and the investor levels, tax depreciation rules, interest deductions, income measurement rules (such as the taxation of nominal capital gains on a realization basis and the taxation of nominal interest), and a given dividend payout policy.

Computed marginal effective tax rates by method of finance are shown in table 4.6. Effective tax rate calculations are provided for a completely leveraged

---

[112] In general, dividends and capital gains received by individuals (directly or through pass-through businesses) are currently taxed at a maximum rate of 15 percent, while interest is taxed as ordinary income at rates up to 35 percent.

[113] Because of the time value of money, the ability to defer taxes lowers the real cost. It is customary to assume that deferral reduces the effective burden on the capital gains tax rate by about one-half.

[114] An additional tax advantage accrues to debt-financed investment because the tax system does not adjust interest flows for the effects of inflation. See the discussion in Mackie (2002).

[115] See Gordon and Malkiel (1981) for a discussion of the costs of increased risk of financial distress and bankruptcy.

investment and for an investment where only equity is used. In order to highlight the tax differences, these estimates do not reflect differences in non-tax costs under the alternative financing methods. Table 4.6 clearly illustrates the strong tax bias towards debt under the current business tax system.

Table 4.6. The Current Tax System Heavily Favors Debt Finance

Method of Finance	Marginal Effective Tax Rates
	Percent
Debt-Financed Investment	-2.2
Equity-Financed Investment*	39.7

*The equity-financed investment is assumed to be partly financed with retained earnings and partly with new equity, reflecting a historical dividend/earnings payout percentage.

Source: U.S. Department of the Treasury, Office of Tax Analysis.

Approaches for Addressing the Tax Bias that Favors Debt Finance

Reduce the Tax Burden on Equity

One way to level the playing field between debt and equity financing would be to reduce the tax burden on equity-financed investment by allowing a dividend exclusion.[116] This approach would exempt shareholder-level dividends from tax. To the extent that the dividend tax, rather than the capital gains tax, burdens the return on corporate equity- financed investment,[117] this approach would dramatically reduce the tax differential between debt and equity.[118]

---

[116] See U.S. Department of the Treasury (1992), chapter 2, for a detailed discussion of a dividend exclusion proposal.

[117] There are two prominent views on the extent to which the dividend tax burdens the return on a marginal corporate equity-financed investment. Under the traditional view, the dividend tax acts as a heavy burden on marginal investment. In contrast, under the new view, the dividend tax acts to reduce the value of corporate shares, rather than to reduce the tax incentive to invest, and so imposes little, if any, burden on marginal corporate investment. It is unclear which view most accurately represents the tax incentives faced by the typical corporation. Available empirical evidence suggests that some firms might operate on each margin (Auerbach and Hassett, 2003).

[118] This approach would reverse the existing tax difference between dividends and capital gains on retained earnings. It also is likely to reduce the size of the difference, thereby reducing the tax penalty on dividends (under the traditional view) and on new share issues (under the new view).

Reduce the Tax Advantage for Corporate Debt

An alternative and somewhat more far reaching approach would be to address the tax bias for debt financing by raising the tax burden on interest income produced in the corporate sector (i.e., the return on debt-financed investment) relative to the tax burdens on distributed and retained earnings (i.e., the return to equity-financed investment). This approach could involve:

- Elimination of the deductibility of interest by corporations (other than S corporations);
- Elimination of the taxation of interest received by corporations from other domestic corporations (other than interest received by S corporations);
- Allowance of a 100-percent DRD; and
- Reduction in the maximum personal tax rate on interest income to 15 percent (to synchronize the tax rate with the maximum rate imposed on dividends and capital gains).

By denying the deduction for interest, this approach would subject income from debt-financed investments to the corporate income tax. It would also remove completely any taxation at the corporate level of interest and dividends received from other domestic corporations; the income represented by these payments would have already been taxed at the corporate level. As a result, both interest and corporate profits (whether retained or distributed) would be subjected to the same corporate tax burden.

Because of differences in taxation under the individual income tax, however, this approach would eliminate the tax bias between debt and equity under the corporate income tax only to the extent that the return to equity is taxed as a dividend. To the extent that the return to equity is taxed as a capital gain, and so benefits from deferral (and possibly the tax-free step-up in basis at death), equity would have a tax advantage over debt, whose return (i.e., interest) does not benefit from deferral. The extent of the tax bias, however, might well be smaller than the bias that exists under current law. By taxing interest at a lower rate, this approach would create a tax bias in favor of debt financing for non-corporate businesses.

Without further modification, this approach would increase the marginal effective tax rate on new investment because it would raise the tax burden on debt-financed corporate investment. In this way it differs fundamentally from the approach of allowing shareholders to exclude dividends, which would lower the marginal effective tax rate on new investment. This approach could, of course, be combined with other options to lower the effective tax rate on corporate investment, such as lowering the corporate tax rate or providing faster write-offs of investment. In addition, by lowering the tax rate on interest income, the approach would reduce somewhat the marginal effective tax rate on non-corporate business investment and on owner-occupied housing, to the extent that such investment is financed by borrowing. This would tend to increase the tax bias against investment in the corporate sector, but would also partially offset any increase in the overall economy-wide marginal effective tax rate.

This approach would create some compliance and administrative complexities. For example, corporations and tax authorities would need to distinguish between interest income received by corporations from other domestically taxed corporations and interest income received from other entities.[119] In addition, interest would need to be carefully distinguished from rent or royalty income. Under current law, such rent and royalty income is taxed similarly to interest income. Under this approach, however, rents and royalties would be taxed at a higher rate (unless the recipient were tax-exempt), but they would be deductible expenses at the corporate level. Thus, the approach would put increased pressure on current rules designed to classify income correctly.

Financial institutions often earn substantial interest income from their holdings of corporate securities – interest that would not be taxed under this approach. This income would be used to pay non-deductible interest expense to depositors and other providers of borrowed funds, in addition to paying deductible wages and other costs associated with providing specific financial services. Under this approach, such firms could be left with a permanently negative tax base because of their non-interest expenses such as the cost of computers, utilities, and bank facilities. Existing tax rules allow operating losses to be carried backward or forward, but such a solution fails altogether if net taxable amounts are permanently negative. Such financial institutions could merge with other enterprises possessing positive tax liabilities in order to be able to obtain the tax value of the measured expenses – but such a solution means that merger activity would be tax-driven, and possibly inefficient. Financial institutions could also possibly recharacterize a portion of interest income received from corporate sources as taxable fees-for-services (which would be deductible to the payor corporations), but the extent to which this could or would occur is uncertain. Other self-help would be available in the form of substituting taxable credit market securities

---

[119] Interest received by corporations from the U.S. government, homeowners, non-corporate businesses, S corporations, and foreign corporations without effectively connected U.S. income would continue to be taxed at the corporate level under this approach.

(i.e., Treasury bonds, home mortgages, and foreign corporate bonds) for domestic corporate debt securities.[120]

C. TAXATION OF INTERNATIONAL INCOME

As discussed in Chapter III, the current U.S. system for taxing international income is a hybrid, containing elements of both worldwide and territorial systems. Generally, U.S. corporations are taxed on all their income whether earned in the United States or abroad; that is, corporations are taxed on their income on a worldwide basis. However, U.S. parent corporations with foreign subsidiaries are generally not taxed by the United States on the active business income of their foreign subsidiaries until such income is repatriated as a dividend. Until that time, U.S. tax on that foreign source income is generally deferred, subject to anti-deferral rules. To alleviate the double taxation of foreign income, the United States allows a credit against U.S. tax for foreign taxes paid. The foreign tax credit is generally limited to the U.S. tax liability on a taxpayer's foreign source income in a particular category.

1. Subpart F anti-deferral rules

Background

The deferral of U.S. taxation of the earnings of foreign subsidiaries is limited by certain anti-deferral regimes, such as subpart F (so named for its place in the Internal Revenue Code), which impose current U.S. taxation on certain types of income earned by certain foreign corporations.

The subpart F rules apply to controlled foreign corporations (CFCs) and their U.S. shareholders. Generally, a foreign corporation is a CFC if more than 50 percent of the vote or value of the corporation's stock is owned (directly, indirectly, or constructively) by U.S. persons that own at least 10 percent of the voting stock of the corporation (U.S. shareholders). Each U.S. shareholder must currently include in income for U.S. purposes its pro rata share of the CFC's subpart F income, regardless of whether the income is distributed by the CFC. Subpart F income generally includes passive and other types of highly mobile income, including so-called "foreign base company income," which includes dividends, interest,

---

[120] These issues regarding financial institutions also arise in the context of instituting a value-added tax or other consumption-based taxes. See Chapter II.

rents, and royalties, as well as income from certain sales and services transactions with related parties.

The Changing Economic Context in which the Anti-Deferral Rules Operate

Subpart F was enacted in the early 1960s, at a time when U.S. policymakers became concerned that U.S. multinational corporations were shifting their operations offshore to defer, or even avoid, U.S. income tax. The dominant position of the United States in global markets at that time made competition between foreign multinationals and U.S.-based multinationals relatively unimportant in considering international tax policy.

Subpart F represented a compromise that eliminated deferral for passive investment income as well as income generated through so-called "foreign base companies" that were thought to shift income from manufacturing and selling products and from services out of the country in which the actual business activity took place to a lower-tax jurisdiction. In an environment where the United States was the world's globally dominant economic power, subpart F was enacted to prevent "deflection" of income to low-tax jurisdictions not only from the United States, but also from other high- tax developed countries. Forty-five years after it was first enacted, subpart F remains the centerpiece of U.S. taxation of cross-border corporate income.

The emergence of a more integrated global economy and changes in the position of the United States within that global economy may have eroded the economic policy rationale for concern with deflection of income from high-tax developed countries to low-tax jurisdictions. The United States is less economically dominant today than it was when subpart F was enacted. In 1960, the United States accounted for 34 percent of worldwide output.[121] In 2006, the United States accounted for only 27.4 percent of worldwide output. In 1960, 18 of the world's 20 largest companies ranked by sales were U.S. companies. By 2006, that number had fallen to 10. The U.S. share of total worldwide outbound foreign direct investment (FDI) fell from 36 percent in 1980 to 19 percent in 2006.[122] By almost any measure, the United States today is less economically dominant than it was 45 years ago.

---

[121] Thomas (2001) reported that the United States accounted for half of the world's total gross national product in 1947, and that this percentage declined to 34 percent in 1960.

[122] The U.S. share of world output is from the World Bank website. The largest companies are from the Forbes website "Forbes 2000" list of largest companies. Data on the U.S. share of FDI are from the United Nations Conference on Trade and Development (UNCTAD) website.

At the same time that the United States has become less economically dominant, U.S. prosperity has become increasingly tied to the success of U.S. business in the global economy. The U.S. economy is much more reliant on cross-border trade and investment today than it was 45 years ago, in large measure because of the growth of other economies around the world. U.S. multinational groups' sales and income from foreign operations have grown much more rapidly than sales and income from domestic operations over the last 20 years. According to the Bureau of Economic Analysis, between 1988 and 2004, U.S. multinational groups' sales made through majority-owned foreign affiliates increased from 33 percent to 47 percent of parent sales. Over this period, sales made through majority-owned foreign affiliates increased 254 percent, while parent sales increased only 147 percent.[123] The reduced U.S. dominance in the world economy combined with the increase in international trade and increasing foreign share of sales of U.S. multinational groups mean that the importance of U.S. competitiveness to the well-being of U.S. companies, workers, and investors has increased over time and likely will continue to increase.

In addition, in an environment where the most relevant competitors of U.S. multinational corporations are non-U.S. multinational corporations rather than other U.S. multinational corporations, U.S. international tax policy must take into account how nonU.S. multinational corporations operate and are taxed. Growing cross-border trade and investment have increased the legitimate need for multinational groups to manage their overseas activities through regional management and finance centers, and to move products, services, and funds across a global structure in a coordinated and efficient manner. Moreover, 1960s-era concerns about deflection of income from other high-tax countries to low-tax countries may now be less relevant for U.S. tax policy both because of the increased use by other countries of measures to combat income deflection and because of the increased competition U.S.-based multinational corporations face from non-U.S. multinational firms. Thus, it may be desirable to modify the subpart F rules so that U.S. companies may compete more effectively with foreign-based multinational corporations in the global economy.

---

[123] See http://www.bea.gov/newsreleases/international/mnc/mncnewsrelease.htm

Approaches for Modifying Subpart F Anti-Deferral Rules

Amend the Foreign Base Company Sales and Services Rules for Certain Sales and Services between CFCs and Related Parties

Under this approach, the foreign base company sales and services income definitions would be modified to exclude income from transactions between a CFC and a foreign related party. Thus, for example, a distribution company that purchases goods from a related party in a neighboring country and sells those goods to consumers located in third countries would no longer have foreign base company sales income as a result of those activities. This approach would allow U.S. multinational corporations to structure their overseas services and distribution networks more efficiently. The rules relating to foreign base company sales and services income would otherwise remain unchanged and thus the rules with respect to U.S.-to-foreign transactions would remain as a backstop to prevent the U.S. tax base from being shifted to low- or no-tax jurisdictions.

Make Permanent the Current Temporary Subpart F "Look-through" Rules for Dividends, Interest, Rents, and Royalties Paid between Related CFCs

Current law provides a temporary exception from certain foreign base company income rules for certain dividends, interest, rents, and royalties received or accrued by one CFC from another CFC that is a related person. The temporary "look-through" exception applies to taxable years of foreign corporations beginning after December 31, 2005, and before January 1, 2009, and to taxable years of U.S. shareholders with or within which such taxable years of the foreign corporations end. This approach would make the current temporary rule permanent, allowing U.S. multinational corporations to fund and to operate their overseas groups more efficiently.

Make Permanent the Current "Active Financing" Exception for Certain Income Earned in Banking, Financing, or Insurance Business

The "active financing" exception provides that qualified banking or financing income of an eligible CFC and qualified insurance income of a qualified CFC generally is not subpart F income. The exceptions apply to taxable years of foreign corporations beginning after December 31, 1998, and before January 1, 2009, and to taxable years of U.S. shareholders with or within which such taxable years of the foreign corporations end. This approach would make the temporary active financing exception permanent, giving U.S. financial services companies needed certainty.

2. Simplifying Foreign Tax Rules for Small Businesses

Globalization brings more U.S. businesses into the global economy each year. As a result, provisions such as subpart F, which was originally intended to affect large multinational corporations almost exclusively, increasingly affect small and medium- sized U.S. businesses. Moreover, the complexity of the foreign tax credit and anti- deferral rules can create costly compliance and enforcement challenges. Notwithstanding the policy considerations that may continue to weigh in favor of maintaining a subpart F regime or foreign tax credit limitations, some relief may be appropriate for those U.S. businesses that incur relatively small amounts of foreign income and foreign tax, to lower the tax barriers that exist to entering global markets.

Approaches for Simplifying Foreign Tax Rules for Small Businesses

Increase the Subpart F De Minimis Rule
Subpart F currently provides a rule to exempt businesses with a de minimis amount of certain foreign income. Specifically, subpart F provides that no part of a CFC's gross income for the taxable year is treated as foreign base company income or insurance income if the sum of the foreign base company income and insurance income for the taxable year is less than 5 percent of gross income or $1 million, whichever is lower (commonly referred to as the "subpart F de minimis rule"). Increasing the de minimis threshold would permit smaller companies to earn foreign base company income and insurance income without becoming subject to the complicated subpart F rules. Under this approach, the subpart F de minimis rule threshold would be increased to the lesser of 5 percent of gross income or $5 million.

Simplify the Foreign Tax Credit Rules for Individuals and Corporations that Incur Relatively Small Amounts of Foreign Tax on Their Active Business Income
This approach would permit individuals and corporations that incur no more than $5,000 in foreign tax on their foreign source income attributable to active business operations to credit those foreign taxes without limitation. This approach would allow a taxpayer to elect to eliminate the calculation of the foreign tax

credit limitation if the taxpayer incurs small amounts of foreign tax on foreign source active business income. Individuals could continue to elect to eliminate the foreign tax credit limitation on their foreign passive income for which they paid a small amount of foreign tax.

3. Modifying the Taxation of Americans who Live and Work outside the United States

Background

Under current law, qualified individuals may elect to exclude from gross income a limited amount of foreign earned income and housing costs. The maximum exclusion (the foreign earned income limit) is $87,500 for 2007 and is indexed for inflation. Complex rules apply for determining the maximum amount of the housing exclusion (housing cost limitation).

In order to qualify for the exclusion, an individual must have a tax home in a foreign country and be either: (i) a U.S. citizen who is a bona fide resident of a foreign country for an uninterrupted period that includes an entire taxable year, or (ii) a U.S. citizen or resident present overseas for 330 days out of any period of 12 consecutive months. Foreign earned income is generally compensation earned for personal services performed by the taxpayer. A taxpayer may not claim exclusions, deductions, or credits that are properly allocable or chargeable to amounts that are excluded from gross income under these rules.

U.S. individuals, like U.S. corporations, increasingly cross borders in the ordinary course of participating in the global economy. The current rules governing taxation of their earned income engender substantial complexity tied to the exact location where they work and reside. These rules also frequently result in U.S. individuals incurring a higher overall tax burden than do citizens of other countries, thereby raising the costs of hiring Americans who work overseas and providing an incentive for companies to hire non-U.S. workers. Simplifying and rationalizing these rules would make it easier for Americans working overseas to comply with the complex tax, filing, and payment rules, while also simplifying the administration of those rules by the government.

Approach for Individuals Living and Working outside the United States

Simplify and Modify the Foreign Earned Income and Housing Cost Exclusion

The approach would combine the current foreign earned income limitation and housing cost limitation into a new, higher overall limitation of $200,000 for both foreign earned income and housing costs (indexed for inflation). The approach would eliminate the complex rules for determining the housing cost limitation.

D. TAX TREATMENT OF LOSSES

The U.S. tax system treats corporate income and losses asymmetrically. A corporation pays tax on its income, but does not receive a tax refund for the tax value of its losses. Subject to various limitations, losses generally can be carried back to obtain a refund of taxes paid in earlier years and carried forward to offset taxes in subsequent years. Because of the time value of money, losses carried forward to future years are worth less than losses that are claimed when they are incurred. As a result, a corporation that has a loss carryforward effectively receives only a partial deduction of its losses. Furthermore, some losses that are carried forward have no value because the corporation never generates sufficient income to use them, and they expire unused.

The current asymmetric treatment of loss and gains creates several economic distortions. It discourages entrepreneurial activity and risk taking because the government takes a full share of the income of a profitable investment, but restricts deductions of losses when the investment fails. Loss restrictions create inefficiencies in investment decisions by increasing uncertainties about the tax effects of new investments. For firms with large loss carryovers, the inability to benefit from deductions for accelerated depreciation reduces the incentive to invest compared to a taxpaying firm that can fully use all its deductions. On the other hand, firms with persistent loss carryovers face a low marginal tax rate on the returns from new profitable investments. Firms are unlikely to know their future tax rates and ability to use loss carryforwards with certainty and loss carryforwards may expire unused. The resulting uncertain tax environment and uneven playing field between firms with and without loss carryforwards may result in both lower total investment and an inefficient allocation of the investment that does occur. The current rules for losses (e.g., lack of refundability, limited carryover, character of income, no interest paid on carryovers) also undermine the effectiveness of the tax system as an automatic stabilizer during business cycles by not providing refunds in periods of low economic activity and lowering taxes during periods of high economic activity. Furthermore, the current rules for losses encourage taxpayers to arrange business transactions and to expend resources in tax planning to alter the character of losses and gains to avoid the loss restrictions.

Analysis of data from corporate income tax returns for 1993 to 2003 indicates the significance of loss restrictions. Those data show that: (1) 50 percent to 60 percent of tax losses are used over a 10-year period as a carryback refund or a loss carryforward; (2) 10 percent to 20 percent remain to be used; and (3) 25 percent to 30 percent are never used.[124] Thus, many corporations incur a significant penalty from the present restrictions on tax losses due to their inability to use the loss carryovers in a timely manner.

The distortions created by the present restrictions on losses could be addressed by allowing losses to be refundable to monetize their value in the current year or to allow losses to be carried forward with interest to reflect the opportunity cost of funds and the erosion in real value. The interest payment on losses that are carried forward would offset the decline in the value of unused losses over time, assuming the interest payment equals the opportunity cost of the funds. However, these options might create problems with fraudulent refund claims. Further, eliminating or relaxing restrictions on capital losses would allow taxpayers to "cherry pick" by realizing capital losses but not capital gains, and provide other planning opportunities. Nevertheless, more limited and targeted changes to the current loss rules might help to reduce economic distortions in certain cases, without creating widespread administrative and enforcement problems.

The Current Tax Treatment of Losses

Current law provides different restrictions on the use of losses depending upon the character of the loss (i.e., whether the loss is an ordinary loss from business operations or a capital loss). An ordinary operating loss (usually referred to as a net operation loss (NOL)) typically occurs when a corporation's deductions exceed its gross income. A capital loss occurs when an asset is sold or exchanged for less than its tax basis, which is generally the original cost less any depreciation claimed.

---

[124] Cooper and Knittel (2006).

A corporation that incurs an NOL generally is not entitled to a tax refund. Instead, the NOLs generally can be carried back two years prior to the loss year and carried forward 20 years, without interest, to offset taxable income in those years.[125]

Loss carrybacks essentially allow a corporation to recover in the loss year previously paid corporate income taxes, and loss carryforwards allow it to reduce future taxes. Thus, allowing losses to be carried back and forward provides a form of income averaging. After 20 years, unused NOL carryforwards expire.

Capital losses are treated differently from ordinary losses. Capital gains and losses are taxed upon realization (i.e., the gains or losses are included in the tax base only when the asset is sold). Because taxpayers can generally choose when to have capital gains and losses included in their taxable income, capital losses can only be deducted against capital gains (but not ordinary income). Otherwise, taxpayers would reduce their tax liability by realizing any capital losses each year, while postponing the realization of gains (referred to as "cherry-picking"). Corporations with net capital losses after subtracting capital losses from capital gains can carry the capital losses back to the three years prior to the loss year (provided the capital losses do not cause or increase a net operating loss in the carryback year) or forward for the subsequent five years to offset capital gains. After five years, any unused capital loss carryforwards expire.[126]

Because the realization of capital gains and losses is more discretionary than the recognition of ordinary income and loss, ordinary losses are allowed to offset capital gain income, but capital losses are not allowed to offset ordinary income.[127]

How Are Losses Treated in G-7 Countries?

No G-7 country offers a refund for losses or provides interest on loss carryforwards (table 4.7). All of the G-7 countries, with the exception of Italy, allow ordinary losses to be carried back for at least one year. For the G-7 countries that allow carryback, the number of carryback years ranges from one to three years.[128]

---

[125] The corporate alternative minimum tax (AMT) rules provide that a taxpayer's NOL deduction cannot reduce alternative minimum taxable income (AMTI) by more than 90 percent of the AMTI. Temporary economic stimulus provisions applying to NOLs originating in 2001 and 2002 generally allowed a longer five year carryback period and waived the AMT limitation on NOL use.

[126] For individuals, capital losses can be deducted against capital gains and do not expire.

[127] Individuals may also use excess losses to offset up to $3,000 of ordinary income.

[128] Donnelly and Young (2002) report that eight OECD countries allow businesses to carry losses back to offset prior payments. All OECD countries allow corporations to carry tax

Three G-7 countries allow ordinary losses to be carried forward indefinitely. While a loss that can be carried back may create a refund in the year the loss is incurred, losses that can be carried forward for 20 years or more without interest have a reduced value.

There is considerable variation in the treatment of capital losses among the G-7 countries reflecting differences in their tax and financial institutions. Canada, the United Kingdom, and the United States do not allow capital losses to reduce ordinary income. France, Germany, Italy, and Japan generally treat capital gains and losses the same as ordinary income and losses, and thus ordinary income and capital gains and losses can be offsetting. However, three of these countries (France, Germany, and Italy) do not allow deduction of capital losses from the disposition of qualifying share holdings because these countries provide a large exemption for any capital gains from such sales.

Restricting the use of losses increases the effective tax rate on a new investment, which raises the cost of capital relative to a system that features refundable losses. For example, a start-up corporation may have significant capital expenditures but little initial revenue. If the corporation faces the prospect of a long period of losses before it becomes profitable, the tax benefits from expensing or accelerated depreciation of capital investments would be substantially delayed. The current tax system discourages corporations from undertaking projects that are expected to have many years of losses before they become profitable.[129]

A tax system without refundability also leads to the unequal tax treatment of investment decisions across corporations. Corporations that have loss carryforwards have a low marginal tax rate, and might have a greater incentive to invest than would a taxable corporation facing a higher marginal tax rate. However, the inability to use accelerated tax depreciation deductions can raise the cost of capital and reduce a loss corporation's incentive to invest compared to a corporation that can fully use all deductions. The difference in investment incentives between loss and profit corporations depends on the size and expected duration of the loss carryforward and the degree of acceleration of tax depreciation.[130]

---

losses forward with about two- thirds allowing a 5- to 10-year carryforward, and the remainder allowing losses to be carried forward indefinitely.

[129] Mintz (1988) finds that partial refundability in the sense of only allowing offsets to past or future income can cause non-taxable start-up firms to face much higher effective tax rates compared to their taxable counterparts.

[130] Gendron et al. (2003) find that investment behavior of Canadian firms is sensitive to the firm's tax status. Auerbach and Poterba (1986) find that the presence of loss carryforwards can have a dramatic effect on investment incentives for cyclical industries such as airlines and manufacturers. Cummins et al. (1994) find that U.S. firms without loss carryforwards are

Table 4.7. Tax Treatment of Corporate Losses in G-7 Countries

	Ordinary Losses		Capital Losses		
	Carryback Period	Carryforward Period	Can Capital Losses Offset Ordinary Income?	Carryback Period	Carryforward Period
Canada [a]	3 years	20 years	No	3 years	Indefinite
France [b]	3 years	Indefinite	Yes	3 years	Indefinite
Germany [c]	1 year	Indefinite	Yes	1 year	Indefinite
Italy [d]	None	5 years	Yes	None	5 years
Japan [e]	1 year	7 years	Yes	1 year	7 years
United Kingdom [f]	1 year	Indefinite	No	None	Indefinite
United States	2 years	20 years	No	3 years	5 years

Note: Most countries have restrictions on the use of losses from acquired firms.

[a] Only 50 percent of capital gains (losses) are includible (deductible) from income. Capital losses can only be used to reduce capital gains not ordinary income, unless the loss is attributable to shares or debt of a small business corporation. A small business corporation is a Canadian controlled private corporation that uses substantially all its assets in an active business carried on primarily in Canada.

[b] The operating loss carryback does not result in a direct refund of the tax payable in earlier years. Instead, the company is granted a tax credit that can be set off against corporate income tax payable in the five years following the loss-making year; any balance is then refunded to the company. Capital losses are generally treated as ordinary losses. Under the participation exemption, 95 percent of the gains derived from the disposition of qualifying shares are exempt from tax. Capital losses arising on the sale of a shareholding qualifying for a participation exemption are not deductible.

[c] Losses may only be offset against positive taxable income, to €1million without limitation per year. A positive taxable income exceeding €1million in a year may only be offset against existing tax-loss carryforwards in the amount of 60 percent. Capital gains are, in general, treated as ordinary income and taxed at ordinary rates (except gains from the sale of shares). Capital gains from the sale of shareholdings between corporations are tax-exempt in Germany. Capital losses arising on the sale of shareholdings are not deductible.

[d] If a loss is derived in the first 3 tax years from the beginning of the company's business activity, it may be carried forward indefinitely. Capital gains are generally treated

responsive to changes in the user cost of capital, while firms with loss carryforwards are not. Altshuler and Auerbach (1990) find that partial refundability of tax losses (and credits) causes substantial persistence in non-taxable status and creates marginal effective tax rate disparities between taxable and non-taxable firms.

as ordinary income. Capital gains derived from the sale of participations, however, are taxed at a reduced rate. Capital losses arising on the sale of a shareholding qualifying for a participation exemption are not deductible.

e Capital gains are treated as ordinary income.

f Major changes in the activities of the company may lead to there being a new trade. Any loss carryforward is set off against the earliest available trading profits. Alternatively, a trading loss may be offset against the other income of the company of the same or preceding year and against capital gains of the same year. The set-off against capital gains is restricted to the amount that cannot be set off against the taxpayer's income of that year. Terminal losses may be carried back for 3 years and set off against profits of any description. Any other non-trading income losses cannot be set off against trading profits.

Source: IBFD (2006) and IBFD (2007).

The current rules for losses also undermine the effect of the tax system as an automatic stabilizer, by not providing refunds during periods of low economic activity and lowering taxes during periods of high economic activity.[131] Corporations are more likely to be faced with losses during periods of low economic activity. Allowing loss refundabililty would increase loss corporations' cash flow during downturns and reduce national tax payments. Under current law, corporations are more likely to use loss carryforwards during periods of high economic activity, reducing their tax liability. Loss refundability would eliminate the system of loss carryfowards and thereby lead to an increase in tax payments during peak economic activity. Allowing loss refundability would increase the stabilizing effect of the tax system.

Loss restrictions also can encourage uneconomic mergers, as corporations combine to secure income against which losses can be deducted as a way to monetize the tax value of the losses.[132] In addition, they can encourage taxpayers to expend resources to plan and arrange business transactions in ways that alter the character of losses, for example, to allow losses to be characterized as ordinary losses, rather than capital losses, to offset ordinary income. Taxpayers with unused capital losses may have an incentive to engage in tax planning that generates income characterized as capital gains. The use of complicated tax strategies to avoid loss restrictions also makes it more difficult for the government to administer and enforce the tax rules.

---

[131] The corporate AMT exacerbates this effect. The AMT's limitation on the use of net operating losses make it more likely that corporations will pay additional tax under the AMT.

[132] Certain tax provisions limit the ability of firms to use the prior losses of acquired firms (e.g., section 382).

Approaches for Addressing the Distortions Caused by Loss Restrictions

The economic distortions caused by the current tax rules regarding the use of losses could be addressed by allowing losses to be refundable. Alternatively, the economic distortions could be reduced by relaxing the restrictions on the use of losses, such as by allowing interest on loss carryforwards or lengthening the time periods for loss carrybacks and carryforwards.[133]

Allow Refundability of Losses

Allowing losses to be refundable would increase investment in risky ventures and encourage entrepreneurship, provide more uniform investment incentives, and allow fewer resources to be wasted in efforts to plan around the existing rules. Allowing refundability of losses, however, would raise significant administrative and tax policy concerns. The current rules help to reduce the incentive for taxpayers to claim inappropriate tax refunds by overstating losses.[134] In addition, loss restrictions help to limit taxpayer manipulation of the realization-based system for assessing taxes on capital gains.

A potential argument against refundability is that it would encourage unprofitable or inefficient businesses. This argument is weak on several grounds. The current tax system does not prevent the use of losses from inefficient or uneconomic business activities as long as the taxpayer has positive income from other sources. This argument also ignores the fact that most businesses encounter negative cash flow in the initial phases of an investment, regardless of their overall profitability over time. Any measure of revenues and expenses for a one-year period is unlikely to be an appropriate indicator of a corporation's profitability and of its long-run viability. Finally, refundability by itself does not encourage uneconomic business operations indefinitely because the tax refunds would always be less than the amount of the corporation's pre-tax losses.

Lack of refundability is sometimes justified as a way to limit losses that arise from the use of tax preferences. Loss restrictions, however, are a complicated and inefficient way to limit tax preferences.

---

[133] Because capital gains and losses are taxed only upon realization, the voluntary recognition of such gains and losses means that it would not be feasible to allow net capital losses to offset ordinary income in most cases. It may be feasible to allow capital gains and losses subject to mark-to-market treatment to offset ordinary income.

[134] The experience in OECD countries with refunds on value-added taxes on exports is not encouraging as such refunds have been an important source of fraudulent claims.

The revenue cost of reforms that move toward refundability of losses could be substantial. For example, the current stock of available NOLs is estimated to be over $1 trillion.[135] Nevertheless, to the extent that losses would otherwise be used, the effect on tax revenues would largely be reflected in the timing of payments. The cost of moving to refundability could be reduced by limiting the refunds to losses that occur after enactment and the incentive effects would not be reduced by imposing such a limit.

Alternative Approaches to Full Refundability

Provide Interest on Loss Carryforwards
Under this approach, a corporation would increase the amount of loss carried forward each year by a stated interest rate. Allowing interest on loss carryforwards would mitigate the effect that loss restrictions have on new investments. For losses that eventually are realized, the payment of interest would reduce the tax penalty on risky investments created by the existing loss restrictions because the interest payment would compensate the taxpayer for waiting to realize his loss.

Providing interest on losses, however, does not alleviate the risk of losing carryforwards entirely if a corporation goes out of business. More importantly, under a realization-based system there is a fundamental inconsistency in paying interest on realized losses while not charging interest on deferred gains. This inconsistency could be exploited by taxpayers who cherry-pick losses and engage in other tax planning designed to generate tax losses and would lead to disputes between the taxpayers and the government.

Allow Losses to Be Deducted Regardless of the Character of Income
While current law allows ordinary NOLs to offset capital gains income, capital losses cannot be used to offset ordinary income. Thus, a business with overall losses taking into account both net operating income and capital losses can still end up paying income tax. One approach would be to allow capital losses to offset ordinary income under certain circumstances.

A major reason that current law does not allow capital losses to offset ordinary income is that the realization of capital gains and capital losses is largely discretionary. Thus, taxpayers could reduce taxes paid by realizing only capital losses, while capital gains on assets that had appreciated in value would not be

---

[135] Cooper and Knittel (2006).

realized, and the tax liability could be deferred, sometimes for indefinite periods. Corporations could structure such transactions so as to reduce corporate taxes substantially. To lessen such tax planning, a limited deduction of capital losses against ordinary income could be provided. Allowing a modest amount of capital losses to offset ordinary income, such as $25,000 or $50,000, would be comparable to the deduction of up to $3,000 in capital losses allowed for individuals against ordinary income, and would provide simplification benefits for small corporations with small amounts of capital losses.

Lengthening Carryback and Carryforward Periods

A more attractive approach may be to lengthen the carryback and carryforward periods. Under current law, a significant amount of corporate capital losses expire undeducted because the carryforward period is only five years. The deduction of NOLs is often deferred because the carryback period is only two years.[136] Both issues could be addressed by providing a uniform carryback period of three to five years and a carryforward period of 20 years that would apply for both capital losses and NOLs.[137] This approach would improve the ability of corporations to deduct losses and would not appear to raise significant administrative problems.

E. BOOK-TAX CONFORMITY

Using book income as the basis for measuring taxable business income is frequently cited as a remedy for the complexity of the current corporate tax regime. Tax rules have diverged from financial accounting rules over time due to differing goals for each system. Accounting rules attempt to represent income fairly for investors and creditors, while the tax law seeks to raise revenue while balancing equity and efficiency concerns. Maintaining different reporting systems requires corporations to incur substantial costs to keep two sets of books and reconcile between the two. In addition, many advocates assert that simply changing the tax base to book income could result in a significant revenue-neutral reduction in the tax rate. This section considers the benefits and risks of adopting a single book system for both financial and tax reporting purposes.

---

[136] The Taxpayer Relief Act of 1997 reduced the net operating loss carryback period from three years to two years, while lengthening the carryforward period to 20 years.

[137] The carryback period for NOLs was temporarily extended to five years for losses incurred in 2001 and 2002 by the Job Creation and Worker Assistance Act of 2002.

Book and Tax Income Measures and Their Differences

Book-tax differences have existed for as long as the corporate income tax has existed. To a large extent, these differences reflect the fundamentally different goals of the two income measurement systems. The primary goal of financial accounting is to provide useful information to management, shareholders, and creditors, and the major responsibility of the financial regulators is to protect these parties from being misled through the overstatement of income. The primary goal of the income tax system, in contrast, is the equitable and efficient collection of revenue, and the major responsibility of the Internal Revenue Service (IRS) is to protect the public fisc. In carrying out that responsibility, the IRS is particularly concerned with the understatement of income. It is quite apparent, then, that the goals of the financial regulators and those of the IRS are not always compatible.

The Securities and Exchange Commission (SEC) has the authority to prescribe accounting and other reporting standards for publicly traded firms, but it has generally ceded rulemaking to the private sector, through the Financial Accounting Standards Board (FASB), which was established in 1973 to set accounting standards. Statements of Financial Accounting Concepts No. 1 and No. 2 require that financial accounting provide information useful to investors and creditors in making investment and other decisions about firms.

In contrast to many tax measures, financial accounting does not require uniformity across firms. While managers may have discretion in reporting book income in certain circumstances, recent legislation and pronouncements have limited the discretion granted to firms in an effort to provide better consistency across industries.[138] Nonetheless, managers of firms within the same industry still retain some discretion and may recognize different amounts of revenue or expense to provide more complete information on their firms' unique circumstances to their respective shareholders. Similarly, there can be significantly different treatments across industries. Although the tax system also allows different methods of accounting, financial accounting may allow greater variances when it comes to choosing methods of accounting.

Financial accounting requires more evidence and certainty for recognizing gain contingencies than for recognizing loss contingencies. Once revenues are recognized for book purposes, however, accounting rules seek to match all

---

[138] See, for example, SEC Staff Accounting Bulletin 101, Revenue Recognition in Financial Statements; FASB Interpretation No. 48, Accounting for Uncertainty in Income Taxes; and the Sarbanes-Oxley Act of 2002 (Pub. L. No. 107-204, 116 Stat. 745).

expenses against the revenue they generate in the current period. As such, even contingent losses are recorded when they are probable and estimable. The accounting principles that require businesses to accrue losses sooner than they can recognize gains could permit taxpayers to use their discretion to decrease the tax base.

In contrast, the primary objective of the tax code is to collect revenues to fund governmental expenditures. To enable the IRS to monitor compliance and collection, the tax law allows fewer choices of accounting methods to determine taxable income than are available to determine financial reporting income. For example, the tax law does not allow certain expenses to be deducted when they are estimated for financial accounting, such as reserves for warranty claims and bad debts. Likewise, the tax law does not permit the deferral of income on certain types of sales that have a right-to-return or price protection. Unlike the broad standards for accounting consistency, the tax code requires uniformity across firms.

While the primary purpose of tax law is to raise government revenue, it has also become a means for providing economic incentives to engage in activities deemed to be economically or socially desirable. Thus, the tax law has rules that intentionally reduce net income in certain cases.

Recent Evidence on Book-Tax Differences

Book-tax differences dramatically increased during the 1990s (Chart 4.1).[139] A number of factors – the strong economy, the increasing use of stock options that provided large tax deductions without book expensing, and the combination of tax shelters and special purpose entities driving a wedge between book and tax expenses and income – all contributed to a steady growth in the book-tax disparity by the late 1990s. However, recent evidence suggests that this disparity varies substantially from year to year. Thus, although in the late 1990s it appeared that large amounts of book income were not included in the U.S. tax base, recent variability and institutional changes make it far less certain whether the measures used to estimate the book-tax disparity provide an accurate picture of a forward-looking book-income base as described below.

---

[139] For more detail on the measurement of book-tax differences see Boynton et al. (2005).

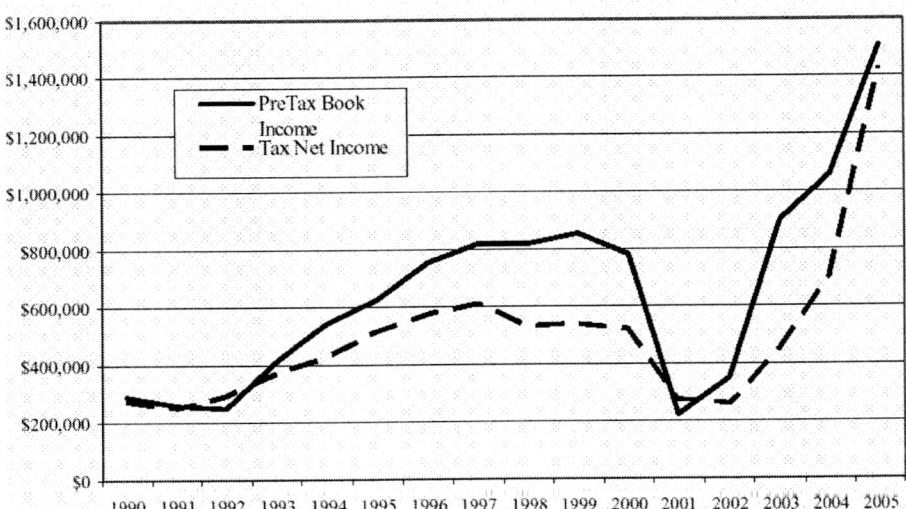

Note: Excludes S corporations, regulated investment companies, and real estate investment trusts. This comparison does not make adjustments for changes in accounting or tax rules. For example, tax net income reflects the impact of bonus deprecation available during 2001-2004.
Source: U.S. Department of the Treasury, Office of Tax Analysis.

Chart 4.1. Pretax Book Income and Tax Net Income for All Corporations, 1990-2005.

Potential Benefits and Costs of Measuring Income Using Financial Accounting Rules

A significant benefit of using book income as the tax base is that corporations would no longer have to keep a second set of books for tax purposes. Eliminating this requirement could save corporations substantial recordkeeping costs and decrease the role of tax legislation and the costs of enforcement.

Going forward the government could build on the massive investment that has been made in measuring corporate income according to Generally Accepted Accounting Principles (GAAP). The expanded apparatus now in place following the Sarbanes-Oxley Act represents a huge societal investment in producing a reliable measure of corporate income. Although the audit failures and reporting errors related to Enron and WorldCom initially focused attention on overstated earnings, the auditing changes imposed by the Sarbanes-Oxley Act and the Public Company Accounting Oversight Board also require more complete audit evidence to support reserves. These changes to improve reliability should make earnings manipulation in either direction more difficult. Sufficient experience does not yet exist to evaluate how resistant book income will be to manipulation under these new rules. As the accounting and tax communities become familiar with reported earnings under these auditing rules, the opportunities for incremental increases in conformity between book and tax income could be explored.

Under a conformed system, a manager's incentive to report more book income to investors is in conflict with the incentive to pay less tax. As such, a conformed system could temper the incentives to engage in aggressive tax planning, including the types of corporate tax shelters that currently purport to generate tax losses without book losses. A conformed system also could temper managers' incentives to overstate income in reports to shareholders, thereby discouraging some of the corporate-governance problems that led to the collapse of Enron and other large corporations.[140]

It is unclear, however, whether the SEC is in a position to protect the tax base from eroding as effectively as it protects shareholders and creditors from overstated earnings. Many corporations might respond to a book income tax base by seeking to decrease book income. Managers might find ways other than official income measures to communicate profitability to investors. If so, new costs might arise related to communicating free cash flow and other pro-forma earnings to analysts, market participants, and creditors. So while tax and book income might be formally conformed, in practice there could be two reporting regimes, one of which will effectively have no formal rules. Thus, it is possible that taxing book income could impair the competitiveness of the flagship financial reporting system that makes the U.S. capital market the strongest in the world, without leading to an increase in tax collections. Indeed, certain evidence from European countries suggests that conformity between book and tax income measures has reduced the reliability of book reporting in these countries.[141]

Moreover, financial accounting has increasingly moved from historical cost accounting toward accrual accounting for assets and liabilities based on their fair market values, with increases and decreases in values recorded as income and expense. Fair value accounting seeks relevance even at the risk of some reliability and certainty. As such, fair value accounting is in stark contrast

---

[140] Desai (2005) provides an extensive discussion of these issues.

[141] Ali and Hwang (2000) and Alford et al. (1993) find that book earnings are less informative in explaining equity returns in countries with book-tax conformity than in the United States.

to tax accounting, which emphasizes certainty and so is based on historical values and the realization principle. Valuation is a judgment call, and the SEC generally does not challenge a firm's valuation if there is a reasonable basis for the value. Using unchallenged financial accounting valuations may place government tax revenues at risk.

Financial accounting also requires more evidence and certainty for recognizing gain contingencies than for recognizing loss contingencies. This rule would tend to reduce tax collections. The accounting principles that require accruing losses sooner than gains also would permit corporate taxpayers to use management discretion to decrease the tax base.

Furthermore, taxing book income would be a fundamental change in how businesses are taxed. As such, there are significant difficulties and uncertainties in developing and moving to such a system. A regulatory and enforcement system for nonpublic firms would need to be developed. Even more importantly, the relationship between FASB/SEC, the Congress, the Treasury Department/IRS, and the federal courts would have to be determined. For example, under a book-tax regime, Congress presumably would no longer have authority over the income tax system other than to set tax rates. In addition, presumably the Treasury Department and the IRS would not have authority to interpret the tax laws, but would cede that responsibility to the FASB and the SEC. It is likely that the process of determining lines of authority and review would be difficult and lengthy. It also seems plausible that over time Congress would gradually reassert itself in the tax policy process, regardless of how clean the break might have been initially. This reassertion raises the possibility that the tax system would then begin to deviate from the financial accounting system, reducing the benefits of conformity.

Revenue-Neutral Tax Rate for a Book Income Tax Regime

In aggregate, book income has exceeded taxable income by 20 percent to 30 percent in recent years. This disparity has led a number of commentators to argue that conforming taxable income to book rules should allow a large reduction in the corporate tax rate while raising the same revenue. Former IRS Commissioner Charles Rossotti suggested that the corporate tax rate could be lowered to 25 percent under such a conformed book-tax system.[142] While a rate of 25 percent seems possible based on simple tabulations of the late 1990s, for

---

[142] Rossotti (2006).

several reasons these calculations do not hold up to closer scrutiny. In fact, the forward looking revenue-neutral tax rate would be substantially higher than 25 percent.

Taking the data that underlies the 25-percent figure above in order to calculate the implied tax rate on book income necessary to match the revenue from a 35-percent tax on net income, results in a rate that would vary between 18 percent and 43 percent over the 1990 to 2005 period. The average rate over this 16-year period is 29 percent.[143] While reflective of recent history, this value may not be informative of a prospective tax on book income. To reflect the anticipated future better, several adjustments are necessary to this 29-percent rate.[144]

First, to forecast future tax revenue, it is necessary to control for aberrations in the historical data. Both bonus depreciation and stock options reduced taxable income without reducing book income. Because bonus depreciation was a temporary policy, it should not be considered part of the baseline tax system. In addition, accounting rules for options have changed so that they now reduce book income like any other labor compensation.[145] Consequently, the historical difference in the treatment of stock options also should not be considered in a forward-looking estimate of the revenue potential of a book-tax base. Controlling for these effects moves the tax and book income measures closer and increases the revenue-neutral tax rate by 3 to 4 percentage points.

Second, book-income measures have been more cyclical historically than tax- income measures. Because of this volatility, estimates are very sensitive to the time period selected for analysis and the composition of the sample of firms. With a long-time series of firms representative of the entire corporate tax filing population, the 1990s do not appear to be representative in terms of the proportion of firms in a loss position. Relative to an aggregate measure of book income, simulations of how losses will offset positive income imply that the revenue-neutral tax rate on book income needs to be increased by another 1 or 2 percentage points.

---

[143] Whitaker (2005) provides an alternative calculation of such a revenue-neutral rate.

[144] McClelland and Mills (2007) provide a more detailed discussion of the necessary adjustments.

[145] Prior to the implementation of Financial Accounting Standard No. 123(R) in 2005, firms could use two methods to expense stock options: (1) intrinsic value accounting under Accounting Principles Board Opinion No. 25 or (2) fair value accounting under FAS 123. Most stock options that vested over a period of time were typically subject to intrinsic value accounting, which had the effect of the firms not needing to recognize any compensation expense. Due to FAS 123(R), companies generally must now recognize a compensation cost equal to the fair value of the equity award on the date of grant. The cost is typically amortized over the vesting period of the award. The fair value of such awards is determined by using an asset-pricing model such as the Black-Scholes model.

Thus, if book income were to become the tax base, the revenue-neutral rate would be between 32 percent and 35 percent, even before considering behavioral responses. It is reasonable to expect, however, that if book income were adopted as the basis for taxation, then reported income would fall for some firms. Most firms currently have incentives to report higher rather than lower book incomes. But once such income is taxed, firms would be expected to use any discretion available to reduce their reported income to lower tax payments and hence increase their after-tax cash flow. While the opportunity and incentives for manipulating book income are uncertain, evidence in the academic literature is consistent with behavior that would require the revenue-neutral tax rate to be increased by a couple of percentage points.

This analysis suggests that the revenue-neutral book-income tax regime would require a tax rate that is not much different from the current tax rate of 35 percent. This system would no longer have accelerated depreciation, tax credits, or any of the other myriad tax incentives of the current system. The recent Treasury Department background paper on business taxation shows that these preferences cost the equivalent of about 8 percentage points of the corporate tax rate.[146] Thus, adding these preferences to a book-income regime could force the revenue-neutral rate to be higher than the current rate of 35 percent.

In summary, the risks from adopting book income as the basis for taxation appear to be substantial. While full conformity might not be an appealing template for business tax reform, policymakers should keep in mind the potential simplification benefits of more targeted conformity.

F. ILLUSTRATIVE AREAS TO IMPROVE TAX ADMINISTRATION

Whether or not major reform of the corporate income tax is accomplished, many specific provisions of the current corporate income tax could be reformed so as to reduce complexity and costs of compliance with the tax system. While this chapter discusses a number of potential areas for reform, this section examines two additional areas for consideration, the corporate alternative minimum tax and simplified cash accounting for small business.

1. Corporate Alternative Minimum Tax

Corporations must calculate their tax liability by applying two sets of rules. Corporations compute their tax liability under the regular tax rules, compute their tentative AMT liability under the AMT rules, and pay whichever is greater. The corporate AMT rules have a broader definition of income and a less generous set of deductions than the regular tax rules. Additionally, the corporate AMT may be credited against future regular tax liability, but the credit may not be used to reduce regular tax liability below the tentative minimum AMT.

The corporate AMT is largely a function of timing. Through the rules under the corporate AMT, a corporation's tax liability is increased currently, but it will likely receive the delayed tax benefits at a future time through the AMT credit mechanism. As a result, the corporate AMT largely results in the deferral, but not elimination, of certain favorable tax benefits.

Corporate AMT Tax Payments

In 2004, corporate AMT payments were $3.4 billion. In contrast, total corporate income tax liability net of credits was $199.3 billion. The total amount of unused AMT credits available equaled $18.8 billion (table 4.8). The AMT credit figure does not include unallowed nonconventional source fuel credits and unallowed qualified electric vehicle credits, which can be added to a corporation's total available AMT credits. Including these credits, the total amount of available AMT credits in 2004 equaled $29.4 billion (table 4.9).[147]

Table 4.9 also shows the amount of AMT credits available by industry in 2004, including unallowed nonconventional fuel credits and unallowed qualified vehicle credits. The industries with the largest amount of AMT credits available in 2004 were manufacturing ($9.9 billion) and finance and insurance ($6.2 billion).

A study of firms in the period from 1995 to 2002 showed that almost 50 percent of the firms paid higher taxes due to the AMT in at least one year, either through direct AMT payments or through limits on the use of tax credits due to the AMT rules. These firms accounted for over 70 percent of all corporate cases examined in this period.[148]

---

[146] U.S. Department of the Treasury (2007).

[147] Prior to passage of the Energy Policy Act of 2005, if a taxpayer was unable to claim the nonconventional fuel credit solely because it would reduce regular tax liability below the taxpayer's AMT, the unused credit increased the taxpayer's AMT credit.

[148] See Carlson (2005a).

Table 4.8. AMT Credit Use, 1987-2004[*]

Year	AMT Payments	AMT Credits	Net AMT (after credits)	AMT Credits Balance
	$ billions			
1987	2.2	-	2.2	2.2
1988	3.4	0.5	2.9	5.1
1989	3.5	0.8	2.7	7.8
1990	8.1	0.7	7.4	15.2
1991	5.3	1.5	3.8	19.0
1992	4.9	2.3	2.6	21.6
1993	4.9	3.1	1.8	23.4
1994	4.5	3.3	1.2	24.6
1995	4.3	4.8	-0.5	24.1
1996	3.8	4.7	-0.9	23.2
1997	3.9	4.1	-0.2	23.0
1998	3.3	3.4	-0.1	22.9
1999	3.0	3.4	-0.4	22.5
2000	3.9	5.2	-1.3	21.2
2001	1.8	3.3	-1.5	19.7
2002	2.5	2.0	0.5	20.2
2003	2.3	3.4	-1.1	19.1
2004	3.4	3.7	-0.3	18.8
Total	69.0	50.2	18.8	-

Note: Data exclude S corporations, regulated investment companies, and real estate investment trusts.

[*] Does not include unallowed nonconventional source fuel credit and unallowed qualified electric vehicle credit.

Source: Internal Revenue Service, Statistics of Income, Corporate Tax Returns, 1993-2004.

Table 4.9. Total Corporate AMT Credits Outstanding by Industry in 2004*

Industry	Total AMT Credits Outstanding at End of Year $ millions
Agriculture, Forestry, Fishing, and Hunting	50
Mining	2,382
Utilities	3,824
Construction	235
Manufacturing	9,931
Wholesale and Retail Trade	1,888
Transportation and Warehousing	1,820
Information	1,070
Finance and Insurance	6,153
Real Estate and Rental and Leasing	529
Professional, Scientific and Technical Services	294
Management of Companies (Holding Companies)	467
Administrative and Support and Waste Management and Remediation Services	285
Education Services	6
Health Care and Social Assistance	95
Arts, Entertainment, and Recreation	52
Accommodation and Food Services	342
Other Services	18
Total	29,441

Note: Data exclude S corporations, regulated investment companies, and real estate investment trusts. *Includes unallowed nonconventional source fuel credit and unallowed qualified electric vehicle credit.
Source: Internal Revenue Service, Statistics of Income Corporate Tax Returns, 2004.

Economic Effects of the Corporate AMT

In addition to its financial effects, the corporate AMT may reduce a firm's investment incentives. In general, deductions for investment projects are taken at a slower rate under the AMT, increasing a firm's cost of capital.[149] The AMT might also lessen investment by reducing a firm's cash flow, thereby forcing some corporations to finance investment with costly external funds. The after-tax cost of debt financing is also increased when a firm is paying AMT since interest is deducted at a lower rate than for regular tax purposes. In addition, the AMT reduces the ability of a firm to claim most business tax credits, such as the research and experimentation credit, and may restrict the firm's ability to claim NOL deductions and foreign tax credits. These restrictions may cause the benefit of these credits to be lost permanently if they cannot be used during the carryforward period.

Moreover, the corporate AMT is pro-cyclical. It tends to impose an increased tax burden during an economic downturn, which may result in deeper and prolonged economic weakness by reducing business activity. A study of the AMT found that the odds of a corporation being affected by the AMT increase when the economy slows down. For a 1-percentage point decrease in GDP growth, the odds of being affected by the AMT increase by 7 percent or 0.5 percentage points.[150]

A company that hires more workers is also likely to increase its chances of being an AMT taxpayer during periods of low profitability. Any activity that reduces net income (such as keeping employees on the payroll during periods of low demand or increasing investment) increases the likelihood of paying AMT because AMT adjustments and preferences become larger relative to the company's net income.

Some may argue that the corporate AMT ensures that corporations pay their fair share of taxes and do not receive disproportionate benefits from special tax provisions. Without the corporate AMT, some corporations would pay no corporate income tax. A study of 2002 tax data, for example, revealed that about 47 percent of firms with positive AMT payments were in a loss situation for regular tax purposes.[151] Reductions in tax preferences, however, would be a preferable approach to limit the ability of firms to avoid taxes through special provisions. The

---

[149] However, revenue generated by an investment by a firm subject to AMT is taxed at a 20-percent rate rather than the top 35-percent rate under the regular tax. The reduced rate of taxation on the additional revenue reduces the cost of capital. The net effect on the firm's cost of capital for marginal investment projects is ambiguous without a detailed calculation of the magnitude of these two effects. Whether a firm is in tax-profit status or tax-loss status will also have an effect on the cost of capital. Relative to tax-loss status of equal duration, the AMT cost of capital can be either higher or lower.

[150] See Carlson (2005a).

[151] See Carlson (2005a).

corporate AMT is an unnecessarily complex approach for reducing the effects of tax preferences and can affect overall corporate competitiveness.[152]

The corporate AMT makes corporations perform the expensive and burdensome task of complying with two separate tax systems without raising any significant revenue.[153] In 2002, over 13,000 corporations had their taxes increased by the AMT. These 13,000 companies account for a significant amount of total business activity, and they held almost 24 percent of all corporate assets. Even those firms not directly affected by the AMT incurred the extra costs of calculating their tax liability and planning for investments under both the regular tax system and the AMT system. At the same time, the corporate AMT, net of AMT credits claimed for prior year AMT, has raised virtually no revenue over the past several years.

The corporate AMT (unlike the individual AMT) is no longer a significant source of revenue and would be unnecessary as part of a broad tax reform that eliminated the various special business tax provisions. In 2004, corporate AMT receipts equaled $3.4 billion while AMT credits equaled $3.7 billion. Annual net minimum taxes (AMT payments minus AMT credits) have been positive only once since 1995. However, in 2004 there were $29.4 billion in AMT credits that were carried forward to 2005. These carryover credits would have to be addressed as part of any major change to the business tax system.

2. Simplified Cash Accounting for Small Businesses

Studies of the tax-compliance burden imposed on business consistently find that small firms bear a larger burden relative to their size than do larger firms.[154] One approach for simplifying the recordkeeping burden imposed on small taxpayers without encouraging tax avoidance and causing revenue losses would be to permit simpler accounting methods such as the limited use of "simplified cash accounting" by small business taxpayers. Simplification could also permit full expensing of depreciable property, other than buildings, for certain small businesses. Such simplification would go well beyond the

---

[152] In addition, some argue that there is little to support the idea that corporations should necessarily be required to pay some minimum amount of taxes for reasons of fairness. For a detailed discussion, see Lyon (1997).

[153] Researchers have found that being subject to the corporate AMT raises compliance costs by about 11 percent to 17 percent. See Slemrod and Ventakash (2002) and Slemrod (1997).

[154] Slemrod and Venkatesh (2004), and Moody (2002).

current cash-accounting rules in reducing the burden of tax compliance on many small businesses.

Compliance Burden of Small Businesses

Research on the tax-compliance costs of small, medium, and large firms have at least two findings in common: (1) total costs of compliance rise with the size of the business, but (2) costs relative to size (e.g., per employee or as a percentage of assets) fall as size increases. With a significant amount of fixed costs, the compliance burden, therefore, is sometimes described as being "regressive."

As an example of these findings, table 4.10 provides results from a study of small partnerships, S corporations, and C corporations (under $10 million in assets) in 2003 and 2004, the only systematic study of tax compliance costs of small businesses in the United States.[155] The table presents results for the authors' "high" and "low" estimates of annual time and money burden, and an aggregate estimate with time monetized at $25 per hour.

Both average time and money spent on tax compliance rise with the size of the firm. However, relative to assets, both money burden and total burden with time monetized fall as asset size increases. These qualitative conclusions are robust with other measures of size examined, and other monetization rates. The authors interpret the results as suggesting that "small businesses face significant fixed compliance costs combined with decreasing marginal costs as the business grows."[156] This suggestion is bolstered by the authors' survey results, which show that the vast majority of time burden (85 percent) is spent in recordkeeping activities, of which accounting is a part.

In addition to being a burden on taxpayers, recordkeeping and accounting are compliance problems for the IRS. Compliance data from the National Research Program (NRP) for 2001 show, for example, an error rate on cost of goods sold for sole proprietorships of over 50 percent, one of the highest error rates for items on the Schedule C (the sole proprietorship tax return).[157] The NRP data do not indicate why errors were made – whether they reflect intentional noncompliance or inadvertent errors that could result from any number of factors, including tax law complexity, poor recordkeeping, or inadequate accounting skills. Nor do the error rates indicate whether amounts were placed on

---

[155] DeLuca et al. (2007).
[156] DeLuca et al. (2007), p. 27.
[157] The error rate is the number of returns with errors on a particular item (in this case, the cost of goods sold) divided by the number of returns on which the item should have been reported. The statistics are taken from unpublished preliminary data from the IRS.

the wrong line because of confusion or lack of attention on the part of the taxpayer. At a minimum, however, a high error rate on cost of goods sold suggests a compliance challenge for both the IRS and the taxpayer.

Table 4.10. Tax Compliance Burden by Asset Size, 2003 and 2004: Annual Average and as Percent of Assets (High and Low Estimates)

Size of Total Assets	Time Burden		Money Burden		Money Burden		Time and Money Burden (Time Monetized at $25/hr)	
	Average (Hours)		Average (Dollars)		Percent of Assets		Percent of Assets	
	Low	High	Low	High	Low	High	Low	High
$0 or Less	199	233	1,301	1,430	n.a.	n.a.	n.a.	n.a.
Less than $10,000	168	203	1,325	1,651	35.1	43.7	146.6	178.3
$10,000 - $20,000	156	159	1,694	1,767	11.6	12.1	38.3	39.3
$20,000 - $50,000	200	229	1,715	1,897	5.0	5.5	19.6	22.2
$50,000 to $100,000	206	212	1,991	2,131	2.7	2.9	9.8	10.2
$100,000 - $500,000	258	262	2,142	2,237	0.9	0.9	3.6	3.7
$500,000 - $1 million	249	263	2,996	3,295	0.4	0.5	1.3	1.4
Over $1 million	419	439	4,025	4,486	0.1	0.1	0.4	0.5
All Businesses	236	255	2,068	2,266	0.4	0.5	1.6	1.8

Note: Based on a representative sample of tax returns filed by corporations and partnerships with assets under $10 million in 2003 and 2004.
Source: DeLuca *et al.* 2007. Tables 10 and 13.

Current Law Accounting by Small Businesses

At present, most unincorporated small businesses are eligible to use the cash receipts and disbursements method of accounting for income and expenses ("cash accounting"). Corporations (other than S corporations) and partnerships with a corporation as a partner can use the cash accounting method only if they have $5 million or less in average gross receipts.[158] Under the cash method,

---

[158] Average gross receipts are computed using the taxpayer's gross receipts reported in the immediately preceding three taxable years. For a member of a controlled group, the group's gross receipts

amounts are generally included in gross income in the taxable year in which they are actually or constructively received. Generally, allowable expenses (except certain expenditures such as inventories and capital expenditures) are taken into account in the taxable year in which they are paid.

Accounting for inventories must conform as nearly as possible to the best accounting practice in the taxpayer's trade or business, and the method must clearly reflect income. For manufacturers, both direct and indirect production costs must be taken into account in the computation of inventory costs. In addition, so-called uniform capitalization rules require that additional indirect costs be capitalized into inventory. A number of exceptions exist for small businesses, however. For example, a taxpayer with property for resale with $10 million or less in average gross receipts who acquires personal property for resale is not required to capitalize labor and overhead costs under the uniform capitalization rules. Also, certain small businesses may use a simplified method of inventory accounting.[159] Under this method, the costs of raw materials purchased for use in producing finished goods and the costs of merchandise purchased for resale are capitalized when purchased. Such costs are generally deducted in the year the finished goods or merchandise are sold. The costs of direct production labor and all indirect costs are deducted when paid.

The costs of property used in a trade or business must, as a general rule, be capitalized and recovered through specified depreciation deductions. However, many small businesses are allowed to deduct up to $125,000 (in 2007) of the cost of equipment, including computer software and most tangible depreciable property other than buildings, in the taxable year the property is placed in service. (This is known as section 179 small business expensing.) The $125,000 limitation is reduced by the amount by which the taxpayer's annual cost of eligible property exceeds $500,000.[160]

---

must be taken into account. Tax shelters are also not allowed to use the cash method of accounting for income and expenses.

[159] These small businesses include (1) taxpayers with $1 million or less in average gross receipts, and (2) taxpayers with $10 million or less in average gross receipts whose principal business activity is not a specified "inventory-intensive" activity (such as retail or manufacturing).

[160] The $125,000 limit is indexed for inflation for taxable years beginning after 2007 and before 2011, but falls to a non-indexed $25,000 thereafter. The $500,000 threshold is indexed for inflation for taxable years beginning after 2007 and before 2011, but falls to a non-indexed $200,000 thereafter. Computer software is not eligible property for taxable years beginning after 2010. The amount of the deduction also may not exceed net business income.

Simplified Cash Accounting for Small Business

Less burdensome alternatives to the current law accounting requirements on small business would allow many of them to use "simplified cash accounting," such as was advanced by the President's Advisory Panel on Federal Tax Reform in 2005.[161] Under this approach (sometimes referred to as "checkbook accounting"), income for most small businesses would simply equal cash receipts minus cash business expenses, and this would apply to inventories, materials, supplies, and depreciable property other than buildings. Taxpayers would no longer have to calculate and keep track of beginning and ending inventories for tax purposes. Expenses of creating or purchasing inventories would be deducted when the cash flows out of the firm, and sales of inventories would be recorded as income when cash is received. Small business taxpayers would no longer have to defer the cost of certain materials and supplies until used. They also would no longer have to capitalize expenditures for depreciable property (except for buildings).

Simplified cash accounting would reduce the amount of tax-related recordkeeping required of many small businesses. Rather than having to keep one or sometimes two sets of often complicated books solely for tax purposes, small businesses could use the records that they use for business purposes – mainly their bank accounts - for tax purposes as well. By reducing the compliance burden imposed on small businesses, this approach would encourage these small firms and entrepreneurs to use their resources in more productive ways. It might also improve their compliance since simpler rules reduce unintended noncompliance.

Simplified cash accounting could be made available to a wide or narrow set of taxpayers. For those using cash accounting for non-tax purposes, wider eligibility would provide greater relief from burdensome accounting requirements and more resources would be released for more productive activities, possibly contributing to improved competitiveness. On the other hand, more limited eligibility would result in less revenue loss from taxpayers able to accelerate the recognition of expenses, and fewer opportunities for taxpayer abuse would arise. Also, smaller businesses that use "checkbook accounting" for non-tax purposes are most likely to benefit from simplified cash accounting. There would be little or no burden reduction (but potential for tax deferral) for taxpayers using accrual accounting for financial purposes.

Table 4.11 illustrates these tradeoffs. It provides information on the accounting choices under current law of taxpayers who could benefit from simplified cash accounting, those who report either cost of goods sold or

---

[161] President's Advisory Panel on Federal Tax Reform (2005). See in particular p. 95.

beginning or end of year inventories, by gross receipts.[162] It shows that, of the 8.2 million business taxpayers with cost of goods sold or inventories, the vast majority (72.1 percent in column 3, or 5.9 million taxpayers) use the current-law cash method of accounting, including 78.4 percent of those with gross receipts under $1 million. However, the volume of economic activity, such as the amount of cost of goods sold, is highly concentrated among the largest taxpayers. To put this table in context, 80 percent (or $12.9 trillion) of the cost of goods sold by all taxpayers is generated by the largest 0.5 percent of taxpayers with cost of goods sold (those with over $25 million in assets). Overall, taxpayers using the cash method of accounting generate only 5.8 percent of all cost of goods sold (column 5); those with less than $1 million in gross receipts only 2.1 percent, and those with less than $10 million in receipts only 4.6 percent of all cost of goods sold. This suggests that extending simplified cash accounting to taxpayers with limited amounts of gross receipts would make the benefit widely available but would limit the likely revenue cost.

Table 4.11. Taxpayers Reporting Cost of Goods Sold (CGS) or Beginning or Ending Inventories and the Use of Cash Accounting, By Gross Receipts, 2005

Size of Gross Receipts	Number of Returns	Percent Using Cash Accounting	Amount of CGS ($ in billions)	CGS on Returns Using Cash ($ in billions)	% of Total CGS
$1 –<100,000	4,226,829	84.9	51.4	42.4	0.3
$100,000–<500,000	2,209,410	70.6	257.2	168.4	1.0
$500,000–<1 million	674,542	62.9	254.7	123.2	8.0
$1 million–<5 million	802,006	33.4	1,072.7	313.9	1.9
$5 million–<10 million	130,351	40.5	635.2	102.7	0.6
$10 million–<25	88,549	13.1	997.1	106.0	0.7
$25 million +up	64,598	4.5	12,902.1	88.8	0.5
Total with positive gross receipts	8,196,285	72.1	16,170.0	945.4	5.8
Under $1 million	7,110,781	78.4	563.4	334.0	2.1
Under $10 million	8,043,138	73.3	2,271.3	750.6	4.6

Note: Taxpayers include corporations, partnerships, sole proprietorships. Data for corporations are preliminary.

---

[162] The gross receipts measure used in this case is for one year only, whereas gross-receipts limits in the tax code generally use a three-year average.

Source: Office of Tax Analysis, based on unpublished data from Internal Revenue Service, Statistics of Income.

Approaches for Accounting Simplification

Taxpayers under $1 Million in Average Annual Gross Receipts

Provide Full Simplified Cash Accounting

Income would equal cash receipts minus cash business expenses, where expenses include the cost of inventories, materials, supplies, and depreciable property (other than buildings). At 2005 levels of activity, simplified cash accounting for inventories, materials and supplies would have benefited as many as 7.1 million taxpayers.[163] Simplified cash accounting of capital expenditures, including expensing of depreciable property (other than buildings), would benefit approximately 1.9 million more taxpayers (in addition to the 7.1 million that could benefit from simplified inventory accounting).[164]

Extend Simplified Cash Accounting,
Except for Certain Capital Expenditures

Alternatively, full simplified cash accounting could be permitted, while the treatment under current law would continue with respect to depreciable property. (Such costs would be depreciated unless eligible for section 179 expensing). As noted above, this approach would benefit as many as 7.1 million taxpayers.

Taxpayers under $10 Million in Average Annual Gross Receipts

Provide Full Simplified Cash Accounting

This approach is the same as above except with a higher gross receipts threshold of $10 million. Such an expansion would increase the number of positively affected taxpayers, 7.1 million in the first approach above with a gross receipts threshold of $1 million, to as many as 8 million taxpayers who would benefit from simplified treatment of inventories, materials, and

---

[163] See column 1 of Table 4.11, "Under $1 million." As under current law, some taxpayers eligible for simplified cash accounting would presumably continue to choose accrual or other methods of accounting.

[164] The 1.9 million represents taxpayers (without cost of goods sold or inventories) who would be able to expense more property than they are currently expensing under section 179. Source: Office of Tax Analysis calculations.

supplies.[165] Another 85,000 taxpayers (in addition to the 1.9 million above) would benefit from expensing of depreciable property (other than buildings).[166]

Extend Simplified Cash Accounting, Except for Certain Capital Expenditures

As an alternative, the simplified cash-accounting approach could be expanded to taxpayers with up to $10 million in average annual gross receipts, while retaining the treatment under current law with respect to depreciable property. Such costs would be depreciated unless eligible for section 179 expensing. This variation of the approach would benefit as many as 8 million taxpayers.

Extend Current Law Cash Accounting for Income and Expenses, and Provide Simplified Inventory Accounting

An additional alternative would permit cash accounting to be available for taxpayers with no more than $10 million in average annual gross receipts. Such taxpayers would also be allowed to use simplified inventory accounting. Direct costs of labor and overhead for inventories would be deducted when paid. Costs of materials and supplies used to produce finished goods, and costs of merchandise purchased for resale, would be capitalized and deducted when the finished goods and merchandise are sold. The treatment of depreciable property under current law would continue. This approach would provide simplification to about half a million inventory- intensive small businesses and to C corporations and certain partnerships with average gross receipts between $5 million and $10 million.

Administrative Issues with Simplified Cash Accounting

Besides the basic question of the size of businesses eligible for simplification, there are several administrative issues that would need to be considered. Many of these administrative issues already exist under current law. For example, under the approaches outlined above, there would need to be rules for firms that move from one side of the size threshold to the other – can a firm move onto and off of simplified accounting year by year, or once a firm is over the threshold, would it be required to stay off the simplified method forever or for at

---

[165] See Column 1, Table 4.11. The increase of 900,000 equals the number of taxpayers with more than $1 million in assets but less than $10 million, and cost of goods sold or inventories.

[166] The 1.9 million represents taxpayers (without cost of goods sold or inventories) who would be able to expense more property than they are currently expensing under section 179. Source: U.S. Department of the Treasury, Office of Tax Analysis calculations.

least a certain number of years? If a firm can change to simplified cash accounting, what does it do with existing inventories? In addition, aggregation rules would be needed to prevent large businesses from creating smaller units to take advantage of the simplified treatment.

REFERENCES

Alford, A., J. Jones, R., Leftwich, and M. Zmijewski. 1993. "The Relative Informativeness of Accounting Disclosures in Different Countries." *Journal of Accounting Research* 31: 183-223.

Ali, A. and L. Hwang. 2000. "Country-Specific Factors Related to Financial Reporting and the Relevance of Accounting Data." *Journal of Accounting Research* 3 8(1): 1-2 1.

Altshuler, Rosanne and Alan Auerbach. 1990. "The Significance of Tax Law Asymmetries: An Empirical Investigation." *The Quarterly Journal of Economics* 105(1): 61–86.

Auerbach, Alan. 1981. "Inflation and the Tax Treatment of Business Behavior." *The American Economic Review* 7 1(2): 419-423.

Auerbach, Alan J. and Kevin A. Hassett. 2003. "On the Marginal Source of Investment Funds." *Journal of Public Economics* 87(1): 205-232.

Auerbach, Alan, and James Poterba. 1986. "Tax Loss Carryforwards and Corporate Tax Incentives." NBER Working Paper No. 1863. Cambridge, MA: National Bureau of Economic Research.

Becht, Marco and Bradford DeLong. 2005. "Why Has There Been So Little Blockholding in America?" In *History of Corporate Governance Around the World: Family Business Groups to Professional Managers*, ed. Randall Morck. Cambridge and Chicago: NBER and University of Chicago Press.

Bittker, Boris and James Eustice. 2007. *Federal Income Taxation of Corporations and Shareholders. 2007 Cumulative Supplement*. ed. Randall Morch. Boston, MA: Warren, Gorham and Lamont.

Boynton, Charles, Portia DeFilippes, and Ellen Legel. 2005. "Prelude to Schedule M-3: Schedule M-1 Corporate Book-Tax Difference Data 1990-2003." Proceedings of the 98th Annual Conference on Taxation, National Tax Association.

Carlson, Curtis. 2005a. "The Corporate Alternative Minimum Tax: Aggregate Historical Trends." OTA Working Paper 93. Washington, DC: U.S. Department of the Treasury, Office of Tax Analysis.

Carlson, Curtis. 2005b. "The Effect of the 2001 Recession and Recent Tax Changes on the Corporate Alternative Minimum Tax." OTA Working Paper 94. Washington, DC: U.S. Department of the Treasury, Office of Tax Analysis.

Cooper, Michael and Matt Knittel 2006. "Partial Loss Refundability: How Are Corporate Tax Losses Used?" *National Tax Journal* 59(3): 651-663.

Cummins, Jason G., Kevin A. Hassett, and R. Glenn Hubbard. 1994. "A Reconsideration of Investment Behavior Using Tax Reforms as Natural Experiments." *Brookings Papers on Economic Activity* 1994(2): 1-74.

Desai, Mihir A. 2005. "The Degradation of Reported Corporate Profits." *Journal of Economic Perspectives* 19(4): 171-92.

Desai, Mihir. 2006. "Taxing Corporate Capital Gains," *Tax Notes* March 6, 2006: 1079-1092.

Desai, Mihir and William Gentry. 2004. "The Character and Determinants of Corporate Capital Gains," In *Tax Policy and the Economy*, ed. James M. Poterba, Vol. 18, 1-36. Cambridge, MA: The MIT Press.

DeLuca, Donald, John Guyton, Wu-Lang Lee, John O'Hare, and Scott Stilmar. 2007. "Aggregate Estimates of Small Business Taxpayer Compliance Burden." Paper presented at the 2007 IRS Research Conference.

Donnelly, Maureen and Allister Young. 2002. "Policy Options for Tax Loss Treatment: How Does Canada Compare?" *Canadian Tax Journal* 50(2): 429-488.

Fama, Eugene F., and Kenneth R. French. 2005. "Financing decisions: who issues stock?" *Journal of Financial Economics* 76(3): 549-582.

Gendron, Pierre-Pascal, Gordon Anderson and Jack Mintz. 2003. "Corporation Tax Asymmetries and Firm-Level Investment in Canada." University of Toronto, Rotman School of Management, ITP Paper 0303.

Gentry, William and David Schizer. 2003. "Frictions and Tax-Motivated Hedging: An Empirical Exploration of Publicly-Traded Exchangeable Securities." *National Tax Journal* 56(1): 167-195.

Gordon, Roger H. and Burton G. Malkiel. 1981. "Corporation Finance." In *How Taxes Affect Economic Behavior*. eds. Aaron, Henry J., and Joseph A. Pechman, 131-198. Washington, DC: The Brookings Institution.

Hare, Jonathan. 2007. "Corporate Capital Gains Taxation in Europe." Presentation at AEI Conference on Taxing Corporate Capital Gains: Economic Implications and Policy Options, March 23, 2007.

Hassett, Kevin and Alan Viard. 2007. "Taxation of Corporate Gains on Sales of Depreciable Property." *Tax Notes* June 4, 2007: 935-943.

Internal Revenue Service. 2007. "Federal Tax Compliance Research: Updated Tax Gap Estimates for Tax Year 2001." Draft mimeo, table C5, July 9, 2007.

International Bureau of Fiscal Documentation (IBFD). 2007a. *European Tax Handbook 2007*. Amsterdam: International Bureau of Fiscal Documentation.

International Bureau of Fiscal Documentation (IBFD). 2007b. *Taxes and Investment in Asia and the Pacific*. Amsterdam: International Bureau of Fiscal Documentation.

La Porta, Rafael, Florencia Lopez-de-Silanes, and Andrei Shleifer. 1999. "Corporate Ownership Around the World." *Journal of Finance* 54(2): 471-517.

Lyon, Andrew B. 1997. *Cracking the Code: Making Sense of the Corporate Alternative Minimum Tax*. Washington, DC: Brookings Institution Press.

Mackie, James. 2002. "Unfinished Business of the 1986 Tax Reform Act: An Effective Tax Rate Analysis of Current Issues in the Taxation of Capital Income." *National Tax Journal* 55(2): 293-337.

McClelland, John, and Lillian Mills. 2007. "Weighing Benefits and Risks of Taxing Book Income." *Tax Notes* 114: 779-87.

Mintz, Jack. 1988. "An Empirical Estimate of Corporate Tax Refundability and Effective Tax Rates." *Quarterly Journal of Economics* 103(1): 225-231.

Morck, Randall. 2005. "How to Eliminate Pyramidal Business Groups: The Double Taxation of Intercorporate Dividends and Other Incisive Uses of Tax Policy." In *Tax Policy and the Economy*, Vol. 19, 135-179. Cambridge, MA: The MIT Press.

Moody, J. Scott. 2002. "The Cost of Complying with the Federal Income Tax." Special Report, No. 114. Tax Foundation, Washington, DC.

Mundstock, George. 1988. "Taxation of Intercorporate Dividends Under an Unintegrated Regime," *Tax Law Review* 44(1): 1-63.

Myers, Stewart C. 1984. "The Capital Structure Puzzle." *The Journal of Finance* 39(3): 575-592.

President's Advisory Panel on Federal Tax Reform. 2005. *Simple, Fair, and Pro-Growth: Proposals to Fix America's Tax System*. Washington: U.S. Government Printing Office.

Rossotti, Charles. 2006. "Simplifying Taxation of Business in America." Testimony before the Senate Committee on Finance, September 20, 2007.

Sinn, Hans-Werner. 1987. *Capital Income Taxation and Resource Allocation*. Amsterdam: Elsevier Science Publishers B.V.

Slemrod, Joel. 1997. "Measuring Taxpayer Burden and Attitudes for Large Corporations: 1996 and 1992." Report to the Coordinated Examination Program of the Internal Revenue Service. Office of Tax Policy Research Working Paper No. 97-1.

Slemrod, Joel, and Varsha Venkatesh. 2004. "The Income Tax Compliance Cost of Large and Mid-Size Businesses." Discussion paper No. 2004-4, Office of Tax Policy Research, University of Michigan, April.

Thomas, Darryl C. 2001. *The Theory and Practice of Third World Solidarity*. Westport, CT: Greenwood Publishing Group.

U.S. Department of the Treasury. 1992. *Report on Integration of The Individual and Corporate Tax Systems – Taxing Business Income Once*. Washington DC: U.S. Government Printing Office.

U.S. Department of the Treasury. 2007. *Treasury Conference on Business Taxation and Global Competitiveness Background Paper*. Washington DC: U.S. Department of the Treasury.

Whitaker, Celia. 2005. "Bridging the Book-Tax Accounting Gap." *The Yale Law Journal* 115(3). 680-726.

INDEX

1

1986 Tax Reform Act, 187

A

academic, 168
access, 115, 135
accounting, 38, 45, 59, 81, 134, 159, 160, 161, 163, 164, 165, 166, 167, 169, 175, 176, 178, 179, 180, 182, 183, 184
accounting standards, 160
ad hoc, 31
adjustment, 62
administration, 111, 147
administrative, 4, 36, 39, 63, 66, 102, 105, 106, 135, 139, 150, 156, 159, 184
AEI, 70, 108, 186
affiliates, 92, 100, 143
aggregation, 184
agriculture, 119
aid, 49, 51, 77, 91, 94, 128
alternative, 26, 53, 76, 81, 85, 90, 95, 105, 106, 121, 134, 136, 137, 150, 167, 169, 183, 184
alternative minimum tax (AMT), 150, 169
alternatives, 179
Amsterdam, 32, 187, 188

AMT, 150, 155, 169, 170, 171, 172, 173, 174, 175
analysts, 165
arbitrage, 134
argument, 61, 157
ash, 184
Asia, 32, 187
assets, 12, 26, 36, 45, 46, 47, 75, 78, 85, 87, 88, 89, 95, 99, 100, 101, 103, 104, 107, 113, 114, 115, 117, 118, 119, 120, 121, 123, 127, 131, 135, 154, 158, 165, 175, 176, 178, 181, 183
assumptions, 52, 89, 90, 95, 121
attractiveness, 79
auditing, 127, 164
Australia, 17, 28, 29, 65, 66, 67
Austria, 17, 28, 29, 66, 67
authority, 38, 160, 166
automobiles, 39
averaging, 150
avoidance, 86, 95, 104, 117, 127, 134, 175

B

bank account, 180
banking, 145
bankruptcy, 135
barriers, 2, 145
behavior, 52, 77, 85, 98, 153, 168
behavioral effects, 122

Belgium, 17, 28, 29, 66, 67
benefits, 4, 5, 15, 37, 40, 44, 45, 47, 64, 75, 76, 80, 83, 84, 85, 89, 92, 121, 124, 138, 152, 158, 159, 166, 169, 170, 174
bias, 4, 21, 84, 111, 112, 124, 133, 135, 136, 137, 138
bonds, 12, 118, 140
bonus, 163, 167
borrowers, 50
borrowing, 76, 138
Boston, 185
break-even, 41
buildings, 36, 45, 66, 175, 179, 180, 182, 183
Bureau of Economic Analysis, 33, 143
business cycle, 149
business taxation, 16, 87, 168
buyer, 114, 117, 124

C

Canada, 17, 24, 25, 26, 28, 29, 65, 66, 67, 124, 126, 132, 152, 153, 154, 186
capacity, 11, 31
capital accumulation, 15
capital cost, 88
capital expenditure, 59, 152, 178, 182
capital flows, 14, 54, 55, 56, 84
capital gains, 12, 23, 24, 25, 27, 35, 48, 51, 64, 86, 87, 88, 111, 112, 113, 114, 115, 116, 117, 118, 119, 121, 122, 123, 124, 126, 127, 128, 133, 134, 135, 136, 137, 149, 150, 151, 152, 154, 156, 158
capital goods, 14, 37, 41
capital inflow, 56, 84
capital markets, 54
capital mobility, 19, 55
cash flow, 46, 59, 114, 129, 155, 157, 165, 168, 173, 180
causality, 52
CFCs, 141, 144
charities, 66
China, 22, 23, 25
citizens, 74, 147
classes, 90
Co, 33, 70, 71

Commerce Department, 104
communities, 164
compensation, 37, 40, 44, 49, 50, 147, 167
competition, 16, 19, 114, 141
competitiveness, ix, x, 1, 3, 4, 5, 9, 10, 31, 61, 76, 79, 94, 111, 143, 165, 174, 180
competitor, 115
complexity, 13, 36, 48, 50, 51, 78, 100, 102, 107, 145, 147, 159, 169, 177
compliance, 13, 51, 63, 64, 65, 66, 81, 139, 145, 161, 169, 174, 175, 176, 180
components, 59
composition, 168
computation, 178
computer software, 179
computing, 49
conflict, 94, 164
conformity, 4, 111, 164, 165, 166, 169
confusion, 177
Congress, ix, 7, 117, 134, 166
Congressional Budget Office, 39, 52, 61, 63, 64, 69, 71
consumer goods, 36, 48
consumers, 37, 38, 39, 50, 52, 144
consumption, x, 3, 10, 27, 29, 31, 35, 36, 37, 39, 40, 41, 42, 44, 45, 46, 47, 52, 53, 59, 140
control, 126, 127, 167
conversion, 116, 122
conviction, 8
corporate governance, 12
corporate restructuring, 116
corporate sector, 12, 24, 36, 54, 55, 83, 86, 95, 113, 115, 121, 123, 124, 133, 137, 138
cost accounting, 165
cost of debt, 173
cost saving, 64
costs, 20, 37, 63, 64, 65, 66, 78, 81, 82, 98, 104, 123, 135, 136, 139, 146, 147, 148, 159, 163, 165, 169, 174, 175, 176, 178, 179, 182, 183, 184
costs of compliance, 169
coupling, 79
courts, 166

credit, 24, 26, 38, 63, 66, 77, 80, 82, 87, 92, 99, 112, 117, 124, 128, 130, 135, 140, 145, 146, 170, 171, 173
credit market, 140
creditors, 159, 160, 164
criticism, 52
cross-border, 2, 8, 9, 26, 61, 95, 142, 143
cross-border investment, 95
cross-country, 56
culture, 66
customers, 96
Czech Republic, 28, 29, 66, 67

D

Dallas, 71
dating, 54
death, 12, 138
debt, x, 4, 12, 20, 21, 22, 23, 25, 73, 74, 75, 83, 84, 104, 111, 127, 134, 135, 136, 137, 138, 140, 154, 173
debts, 161
decisions, 1, 2, 8, 11, 12, 20, 21, 24, 45, 46, 56, 75, 80, 82, 83, 85, 105, 114, 117, 122, 148, 152, 160, 186
deduction, 21, 37, 38, 41, 42, 44, 79, 82, 88, 99, 101, 104, 106, 112, 126, 127, 128, 130, 138, 148, 150, 152, 158, 159, 179
definition, 53, 105, 169
delivery, 27
demand, 15, 174
Denmark, 28, 29, 65, 66, 67
Department of Commerce, 9, 33
depreciation, 4, 14, 20, 21, 22, 37, 41, 42, 44, 81, 82, 83, 84, 85, 86, 87, 88, 89, 117, 118, 119, 136, 148, 150, 152, 167, 168, 179
desire, 62
developed countries, 142
direct cost, 85
directives, 131
discount rate, 20
discretionary, 151, 158
disposition, 113, 115, 152, 154
disputes, 158
distortions, x, 31, 36, 39, 40, 45, 46, 48, 73, 74, 79, 83, 98, 104, 113, 116, 121, 122, 123, 124, 128, 148, 149, 156
distribution, 2, 8, 12, 39, 59, 89, 144
dividends, x, 12, 20, 23, 24, 25, 26, 27, 35, 37, 48, 51, 64, 73, 78, 79, 86, 87, 92, 97, 98, 99, 100, 101, 102, 103, 105, 106, 107, 111, 112, 114, 116, 121, 122, 124, 126, 127, 128, 129, 130, 131, 132, 133, 134, 135, 137, 138, 141, 144
domestic investment, 79, 104
domestic labor, 55
dominance, 143
drugs, 45
duration, 153, 173
duties, 27

E

earnings, x, 3, 10, 12, 26, 27, 31, 32, 48, 53, 73, 74, 75, 77, 78, 87, 91, 92, 94, 95, 98, 101, 102, 107, 112, 114, 127, 128, 129, 130, 136, 140, 164, 165
ears, 55
Eastern Europe, 19
economic activity, 36, 41, 74, 91, 149, 155, 181
economic efficiency, 11, 123
economic fundamentals, 45, 80, 85
economic growth, 4, 15, 82, 113
economic incentives, 162
economic integration, 14
economic losses, 11
economic performance, 35, 36, 40
economic policy, 142
economic resources, x, 73, 114
education, 172
elasticity, 121
election, 117
electricity, 40
eligibility criteria, 49
emerging markets, 22
employee compensation, 37
employees, 40, 50, 51, 128, 174
employment, 9, 14, 92

energy, 135
Energy Policy Act of 2005, 170
Enron, 164
enterprise, 23
entrepreneurs, 180
entrepreneurship, 15, 156
environment, 8, 15, 141, 143, 149
equality, 86
equity, x, 12, 20, 21, 23, 54, 73, 74, 75, 83, 86, 104, 127, 134, 135, 136, 137, 138, 159, 165, 167
erosion, 149
estate tax, 12, 24, 112, 115
Europe, 61, 115, 186
European Union, 19, 115
Europeans, 62
evolution, 16
exchange rate, 61, 62
exchange rates, 61, 62
exclusion, 24, 113, 124, 126, 136, 146, 147
expenditures, 59, 161, 178, 180
expertise, 85
exports, 61, 62, 66, 68, 156
extraction, 27

F

failure, 80
fairness, 94, 174
FAS, 167
FASB, 161, 166
FDI, 142
federal courts, 166
federal government, 51, 63, 122
Federal Reserve, 71
Federal Reserve Bank, 71
fee, 50
fees, 51, 139
finance, x, 1, 4, 8, 20, 22, 45, 51, 73, 74, 75, 76, 111, 134, 136, 143, 170, 173
Financial Accounting Standards Board (FASB), 160
financial difficulty, 135
financial distress, 135
financial institution, 105, 139, 140, 152

financial institutions, 105, 139, 140, 152
financial intermediaries, 50
financing, 12, 20, 21, 75, 83, 84, 96, 135, 136, 137, 138, 145, 173
Finland, 17, 28, 29, 66, 67
firms, x, 2, 14, 15, 22, 73, 87, 88, 92, 115, 120, 128, 131, 133, 137, 139, 148, 152, 153, 154, 155, 160, 161, 162, 166, 167, 168, 170, 174, 175, 176, 184
fixed costs, 176
fixed rate, 95
flow, ix, 1, 13, 40, 44, 46, 48, 49, 50, 81, 86, 87, 114, 128, 129, 155, 157, 165, 168, 173
focusing, 10, 56
food, 40, 45, 65, 96
foreign direct investment, 31, 33, 142
foreign exchange, 62
foreign exchange market, 62
foreign firms, 14, 16
foreign investment, 79, 91
Forestry, 172
France, 10, 18, 24, 25, 26, 28, 29, 32, 66, 67, 102, 106, 126, 132, 152, 153
fraud, 63
fringe benefits, 37, 45
fuel, 170, 171, 173
funds, 59, 98, 139, 143, 149, 173

G

G-7, 18, 21, 25, 26, 113, 124, 126, 131, 132, 151, 153
GAO, 69
gas, 40
gauge, 21
GDP, 9, 15, 16, 21, 22, 27, 29, 30, 47, 51, 174
General Accounting Office, 63, 69
Generally Accepted Accounting Principles, (GAAP) 164
Germany, 10, 17, 18, 24, 25, 26, 28, 29, 66, 67, 126, 132, 152, 153, 154
global economy, ix, 1, 2, 3, 7, 8, 16, 30, 31, 142, 143, 145, 147, 189
global markets, 141, 145
globalization, 9, 91

globalization, 1, 8, 55, 109, 145
goals, 127, 159, 160
goods and services, 2, 8, 9, 27, 28, 37, 39, 46, 50, 55, 62
governance, 164
government, 17, 26, 38, 39, 51, 52, 63, 65, 76, 77, 89, 91, 94, 95, 96, 122, 139, 147, 148, 156, 158, 162, 163, 165
government revenues, 95
grain, 39
Greece, 11, 18, 21, 28, 29, 66, 67
Gross Domestic Product (GDP), 9, 21
gross national product, 142
groups, 143, 145
growth, ix, 4, 7, 8, 14, 15, 51, 52, 83, 113, 142, 162, 174
GST, 38
guidance, 16

H

harm, 124
Harvard, 69
health, 12, 40, 45, 66
health care, 40, 45
heating, 40
heating oil, 40
high-tech, 128
hips, 13, 35, 48, 49, 81, 112, 123, 176, 182
hiring, 85, 147
holding company, 48
homeowners, 139
hospital, 65
hospital care, 65
household, 53, 56
households, 51, 52, 53, 54, 56
housing, 12, 13, 36, 39, 45, 82, 83, 138, 146, 148
Hungary, 11, 28, 29, 66, 67
hybrid, 37, 94, 140
hybrids, 47

I

id, 62
identity, 116
IMF, 70
immigration, ix, 1
implementation, 4, 63, 167
imports, 61, 62
incentive, x, 2, 5, 48, 49, 51, 73, 74, 75, 78, 82, 87, 100, 107, 137, 147, 148, 152, 155, 156, 157, 164
incentive effect, 157
incentives, 36, 78, 83, 102, 119, 137, 164, 168
incidence, 55, 89, 90
inclusion, 84
income tax, ix, x, 2, 3, 4, 7, 8, 10, 12, 13, 16, 21, 22, 23, 24, 25, 26, 31, 35, 36, 37, 40, 41, 42, 46, 47, 48, 49, 50, 51, 52, 53, 54, 55, 56, 57, 58, 59, 64, 65, 74, 77, 81, 84, 86, 88, 89, 90, 91, 92, 94, 98, 103, 111, 112, 114, 123, 127, 128, 129, 134, 138, 141, 149, 150, 154, 158, 160, 164, 166, 168, 169, 170, 174
incomes, 8, 53, 58, 59, 86, 168
increased competition, 19, 143
India, 22, 23, 24
industry, 126, 161, 170
inflation, 20, 112, 135, 146, 148, 179
information technology, 8
innovation, 9, 13, 15, 31, 86
institutional change, 162
institutions, 139
insurance, 66, 82, 119, 145, 146, 170
intangible, 45, 78, 95, 96, 99, 104, 106, 119
integration, 1, 8, 14, 19, 24, 25, 112
integrity, 26
interdependence, 1, 8
interest rates, 77
interference, 11
Internal Revenue Code, 140
Internal Revenue Service, 63, 70, 98, 120, 131, 160, 161, 166, 172, 173, 176, 177, 182, 186, 187, 188
International Monetary Fund, 9, 32, 71
international trade, 1, 8, 9, 55, 61, 143

internationalization, 9
intrinsic, 167
intrinsic value, 167
intuition, 46, 55
inventories, 81, 85, 178, 179, 181, 182, 183, 184
investment incentive, 24, 152, 153, 156, 173
investors, 22, 24, 75, 112, 135, 143, 159, 160, 164, 165
Ireland, 11, 18, 28, 30, 66, 67
Italy, 10, 18, 21, 25, 27, 28, 30, 66, 67, 102, 106, 126, 132, 151, 152, 153

J

Japan, 16, 18, 24, 25, 27, 28, 29, 30, 38, 65, 66, 67, 70, 126, 132, 152, 153
Japanese, 38, 70, 71
Job Creation and Worker Assistance Act, 159
jobs, 92
Joint Committee on Taxation, 61, 70, 100, 108
joint ventures, 115, 128, 133
judgment, 165
jurisdiction, 26, 95, 141
jurisdictions, 99, 100, 107, 142, 144

K

Korea, 11, 28, 30, 65, 67

L

labor, 11, 31, 36, 37, 41, 44, 49, 54, 55, 56, 58, 82, 89, 90, 167, 178, 184
labor productivity, 11, 31, 41, 55, 56, 82
land, 66, 118
large-scale, 25
law, 46, 47, 48, 49, 50, 57, 77, 78, 85, 86, 87, 91, 92, 97, 102, 103, 104, 123, 127, 138, 139, 144, 146, 150, 155, 158, 159, 161, 162, 177, 179, 180, 182, 183, 184
laws, 166

lead, 1, 8, 15, 51, 80, 88, 99, 106, 116, 154, 155, 158
legal protection, 80
legislation, 22, 23, 161, 163
legislative, 3
lenders, 50
lens, ix, 1
lifetime, 20, 41, 45, 52, 53, 59
likelihood, 63, 174
limitation, 92, 146, 147, 148, 150, 154, 155, 179
limitations, 92, 128, 145, 148
limited liability, 48, 49
liquidation, 135
living standard, 5, 10, 11, 15, 31, 36, 41, 55, 56, 82
living standards, 5, 10, 11, 15, 31, 36, 41, 55, 56, 82
local government, 38, 65
location, 2, 8, 12, 95, 96, 104, 105, 147
long period, 152
long-term, 24, 25, 27, 118
losses, 4, 47, 49, 87, 101, 111, 112, 131, 135, 139, 148, 149, 150, 151, 152, 153, 154, 155, 156, 157, 158, 159, 161, 164, 165, 168, 175
Luxembourg, 11, 28, 30, 66, 67

M

machinery, 119
management, 135, 143, 160, 165
manipulation, 156, 164
manufacturing, 77, 81, 82, 92, 119, 131, 141, 170, 179
marginal costs, 176
market, 12, 15, 19, 22, 23, 62, 75, 95, 96, 117, 124, 127, 140, 156, 165
market value, 117, 124, 165
markets, 2, 14, 91
meals, 40
measurement, 40, 81, 136, 160, 162
measures, 10, 21, 28, 29, 53, 83, 143, 161, 162, 165, 167, 176
median, 17

Index

medical care, 40
Medicare, 50
merchandise, 179, 184
mergers, 155
merit goods, 40
metric, 53
Mexico, 22, 23, 24, 28, 30, 67
migration, 99, 106
mining, 119
misleading, 53
MIT, 69, 71, 108, 186, 187
mobility, 19, 55
models, 56
money, 42, 116, 135, 148, 176
mortgage, 140
mortgages, 140
motives, 106
movement, 2
multinational companies, 11
multinational corporations, 9, 77, 78, 92, 94, 95, 102, 106, 141, 143, 144, 145
multinational enterprises, 92
multinational firms, 143

N

national, 16, 25, 33, 83, 96, 126, 132, 142, 155
negative consequences, 104
negotiating, 117
net income, 162, 163, 167, 174
Netherlands, 18, 28, 30, 67
New York, 68, 109
New Zealand, 28, 30, 65, 66, 67
normal, 36, 42, 53, 59, 85
Norway, 18, 28, 30, 65, 66, 67
novelty, 37

O

Office of Tax Analysis, 33, 39, 44, 57, 82, 91, 130, 136, 163, 182, 183, 185, 186
offshore, 100, 107, 141
oil, 40

open economy, 55
Organisation for Economic Co-operation and Development (OECD), 2, 4, 10, 11, 14, 16, 17, 19, 20, 21, 22, 23, 24, 25, 26, 27, 29, 30, 31, 32, 33, 50, 65, 66, 67, 68, 70, 84, 92, 95, 98, 100, 151, 156
ownership, 9, 95, 96, 112, 115, 124, 127, 131, 133
ownership structure, 112

P

Pacific, 32, 187
paper, 1, 33, 69, 70, 71, 109, 168, 185, 186, 188
parents, 92, 98
Paris, 33, 70, 71
partnerships, 12, 13, 35, 48, 49, 81, 86, 112, 115, 123, 176, 177, 178, 182, 184
passive, 36, 48, 92, 101, 105, 141, 146
patents, 45, 78, 118
payroll, 36, 50, 174
penalty, 40, 74, 75, 116, 137, 149, 157
pension, 24
performance, 35, 36, 40
periodic, 115, 134
permit, 32, 88, 146, 161, 165, 175, 184
personal, 48, 49, 54, 119, 120, 137, 147, 178
pharmaceutical, 128
planning, 19, 22, 51, 78, 85, 95, 98, 102, 116, 122, 149, 155, 158, 164, 175
plants, 2
play, 2, 5
Poland, 11, 28, 30, 66, 67
policymakers, 141, 169
poor, 40, 52, 53, 177
population, 168
Portugal, 18, 28, 30, 67
power, 55, 142
pre-existing, 51
premium, 59
present value, 40, 41, 42, 46, 59
President Bush, ix, 7
pressure, 100, 107, 139
prices, 54, 55, 61, 133

private, 77, 154, 160
private investment, 77
private sector, 160
producers, 14, 62
production, 2, 8, 15, 22, 27, 39, 81, 82, 96, 178
production costs, 178
productive capacity, 11, 31
productivity, 11, 14, 31, 36, 41, 55, 56, 80, 82, 115
profit, 42, 59, 128, 134, 152, 173
profitability, 157, 165, 174
profits, x, 4, 12, 13, 23, 48, 73, 74, 86, 87, 88, 97, 112, 138, 154
promote, 11, 80, 85
property, 66, 82, 113, 114, 117, 119, 121, 175, 178, 179, 180, 182, 183, 184
prosperity, 142
protection, 161
public, xi, 59, 66, 111, 127, 160
Public Company Accounting Oversight Board, 164
public policy, xi, 111
public television, 66
pyramidal, 127

R

range, 39, 76
rat, 75, 147
rate of return, 20, 41, 42, 44, 114, 115
raw material, 179
raw materials, 179
real estate, 115, 119, 120, 131, 163, 171, 173
real property, 119
real wage, 54, 55, 56, 92
rebates, 62
recognition, 151, 156, 180
reconcile, 159
recovery, 41, 88
reduction, 3, 4, 5, 44, 46, 56, 75, 76, 79, 83, 84, 85, 87, 88, 89, 133, 134, 159, 166, 180
Reform Act, 10, 16, 113
reforms, 31, 56, 157
regional, 143

regular, 48, 113, 129, 169, 170, 173, 174, 175
regulations, 49, 65
regulators, 160
regulatory requirements, 115, 128
relationship, 52, 56, 95, 166
relevance, 165
reliability, 164, 165
rent, 139
repatriation, 92, 97, 107
resale, 178, 184
research, 52, 54, 56, 57, 80, 99, 102, 106, 122, 173
research and development, 99, 106
reserves, 161, 164
residential, 13, 119
resources, x, 73, 114, 149, 155, 156, 180
responsiveness, 118
retail, 28, 29, 38, 39, 65, 179
retained earnings, 23, 25, 27, 136, 137
retention, 51, 85, 133
returns, 13, 41, 42, 54, 59, 64, 85, 88, 120, 130, 131, 148, 149, 165, 177
revenue, x, 4, 5, 11, 22, 35, 51, 54, 65, 74, 75, 76, 77, 80, 81, 82, 83, 84, 89, 94, 98, 99, 103, 105, 107, 122, 123, 124, 131, 152, 157, 159, 160, 161, 162, 166, 167, 168, 173, 174, 175, 180, 181
rewards, 59, 80
risk, 13, 59, 79, 86, 118, 135, 148, 158, 165
risks, 59, 135, 159, 169
risk-taking, 86
rolling, 124
royalties, 78, 79, 92, 97, 98, 99, 100, 101, 102, 103, 104, 105, 106, 107, 139, 141, 144
royalty, 26, 78, 95, 103, 105, 139
rust, 50

S

safety, 50
salaries, 14
sales, 27, 28, 29, 37, 38, 39, 40, 50, 51, 52, 63, 64, 65, 66, 68, 82, 89, 101, 113, 117, 119, 120, 121, 124, 141, 142, 144, 152, 161, 180

Index

sample, 131, 168, 177
Sarbanes-Oxley Act, 161, 164
savings, 41, 42, 46, 54, 56, 82
securities, 118, 119, 139
Securities and Exchange Commission (SEC), 160
self-help, 97, 98, 140
Senate, 127, 188
Senate Finance Committee, 127
series, 59, 168
service provider, 40
services, 2, 8, 9, 27, 28, 36, 37, 39, 40, 46, 48, 49, 50, 55, 62, 66, 84, 119, 139, 141, 143, 144, 145, 147
shareholders, 48, 54, 87, 114, 129, 130, 138, 141, 144, 145, 160, 161, 164
shares, 59, 101, 112, 114, 115, 119, 126, 129, 137, 154
short run, 14
signals, 12
simulation, 121
simulations, 45, 168
skills, 177
small firms, 175, 180
Social Security, 50
software, 2, 118, 179
sole proprietor, 13, 35, 48, 49, 81, 86, 112, 123, 176, 182
Spain, 18, 28, 30, 67, 68
specific tax, 66, 89
speed, 15
spillover effects, 80
spin, 117
sports, 66
standard of living, x, 3, 74
standards, 12, 15, 55, 94, 95, 96, 160, 162
statistics, 9, 177
statutory, 2, 4, 10, 16, 20, 21, 22, 23, 25, 31, 81, 84, 98, 103, 104, 116, 124, 136
stimulus, 150
stock, 3, 11, 12, 39, 45, 46, 54, 56, 80, 98, 101, 112, 113, 114, 115, 116, 117, 120, 122, 123, 124, 126, 127, 128, 133, 141, 157, 162, 167, 186
strategies, 156

structuring, 85, 122
subsidies, 80
subsidy, 20
substitutes, 96
subtraction, 38
supply, 44, 66, 95, 96
surprise, 90
Sweden, 18, 28, 30, 65, 67, 68
Switzerland, 18, 28, 30, 65, 66, 68
synchronization, 124
systems, 2, 3, 14, 25, 26, 31, 65, 79, 94, 95, 98, 100, 140, 159, 160

T

tangible, 84, 95, 104, 117, 119, 121, 179
targets, 85
tax base, x, 4, 13, 20, 21, 22, 23, 31, 32, 37, 38, 59, 65, 66, 74, 75, 76, 80, 81, 84, 92, 139, 144, 150, 159, 161, 162, 163, 164, 165, 167, 168
tax collection, 165
tax credit, 77, 78, 80, 81, 82, 87, 91, 92, 94, 95, 97, 99, 100, 101, 102, 103, 104, 107, 112, 116, 124, 127, 128, 130, 131, 140, 145, 146, 154, 168, 170, 173
tax credits, 78, 80, 87, 92, 95, 97, 99, 100, 101, 102, 103, 104, 107, 130, 168, 170, 173
tax deduction, 61, 88, 162
tax evasion, 61
tax incentive, x, 73, 74, 75, 137, 168
tax incentives, 137, 168
tax increase, 99
tax policy, ix, 1, 3, 8, 31, 94, 95, 96, 127, 141, 143, 156, 166
tax preferences, 157, 174
tax rates, 2, 10, 11, 12, 13, 15, 16, 19, 21, 22, 23, 24, 25, 27, 32, 41, 48, 55, 56, 63, 65, 74, 77, 80, 81, 84, 85, 86, 87, 91, 94, 95, 116, 117, 121, 123, 124, 128, 133, 134, 136, 148, 152, 166
tax reform, x, 4, 10, 16, 30, 56, 76, 79, 111, 169, 175
tax reforms, 30, 56
tax shelters, 162, 164

tax system, ix, x, 1, 2, 3, 4, 5, 7, 8, 9, 10, 11, 12, 13, 14, 15, 20, 26, 27, 30, 31, 36, 37, 38, 40, 41, 45, 50, 54, 62, 64, 65, 74, 75, 77, 79, 87, 90, 92, 94, 95, 98, 101, 111, 112, 128, 135, 136, 148, 149, 152, 155, 157, 160, 161, 166, 167, 169, 174, 175, 189

taxation, 4, 12, 13, 16, 20, 23, 24, 26, 28, 29, 31, 40, 41, 56, 77, 79, 85, 87, 91, 92, 94, 95, 97, 98, 99, 103, 104, 106, 111, 112, 114, 118, 121, 122, 123, 124, 127, 131, 133, 134, 136, 137, 138, 140, 142, 147, 168, 169, 173

taxes, x, 2, 3, 5, 7, 8, 10, 12, 13, 15, 16, 17, 20, 22, 24, 26, 27, 28, 29, 31, 35, 36, 37, 38, 40, 41, 42, 45, 46, 47, 48, 50, 51, 52, 53, 54, 55, 56, 57, 58, 59, 61, 63, 64, 65, 66, 75, 76, 77, 78, 79, 80, 81, 83, 86, 87, 88, 90, 91, 92, 94, 97, 101, 103, 106, 112, 113, 114, 115, 117, 118, 123, 126, 127, 128, 129, 130, 132, 133, 135, 140, 146, 148, 149, 150, 155, 156, 158, 170, 174, 175

tax-exempt, 24, 139, 154

taxpayers, 13, 24, 38, 45, 48, 49, 58, 87, 97, 102, 149, 150, 155, 156, 158, 161, 165, 175, 176, 179, 180, 182, 183, 184

technology, 82

television, 66

territorial, x, 4, 26, 31, 74, 77, 78, 79, 91, 94, 95, 97, 98, 100, 105, 106, 120, 133, 140

testimony, 127

Third World, 188

threshold, 51, 63, 66, 124, 146, 179, 183, 184

thresholds, 63, 66, 68

time frame, 54

time periods, 156

time series, 168

timing, 157, 170

Tokyo, 70

total costs, 176

total revenue, 123

trade, ix, 1, 8, 9, 14, 55, 61, 62, 63, 105, 142, 143, 154, 178, 179

trade policy, ix, 1

trademarks, 45

trading, 1, 2, 8, 14, 16, 22, 26, 27, 77, 91, 113, 154

trading partners, 1, 2, 8, 14, 16, 22, 26, 27, 77, 91, 113

training, 15

trans, 55, 62

transactions, 50, 61, 78, 85, 98, 100, 113, 116, 117, 118, 120, 121, 122, 124, 141, 144, 149, 155, 158

transfer, 27, 99, 100, 102, 106, 107

transfer pricing, 100, 102, 107

transition, 46, 47, 81, 85, 87, 89

transport, 9, 66

Treasury, 3, 9, 10, 13, 33, 39, 41, 44, 45, 53, 57, 59, 63, 71, 74, 76, 77, 81, 82, 83, 84, 86, 89, 91, 95, 99, 103, 104, 109, 117, 122, 127, 130, 136, 140, 163, 166, 168, 169, 183, 185, 186, 188, 189

Treasury Department, 3, 10, 13, 41, 45, 53, 57, 63, 76, 81, 83, 84, 89, 99, 103, 104, 117, 122, 127, 166, 168, 189

trend, 21

trusts, 120, 131, 163, 171, 173

Turkey, 29, 30, 67, 68

U

U.S. Department of the Treasury, 9, 33, 44, 57, 63, 71, 74, 77, 81, 82, 86, 91, 95, 109, 130, 136, 163, 169, 183, 185, 188

U.S. economy, ix, x, 1, 8, 9, 14, 73, 74, 75, 86, 92, 142

uncertainty, 54, 56, 135

unemployment, 53

uniform, 45, 75, 76, 156, 159, 178

United Kingdom, 10, 17, 18, 24, 25, 27, 28, 30, 64, 66, 68, 126, 132, 152, 153

United Nations, 142

United States, 1, 2, 3, 4, 5, 8, 9, 10, 11, 12, 14, 15, 16, 18, 21, 22, 23, 24, 25, 26, 27, 28, 29, 30, 31, 37, 52, 54, 55, 56, 61, 62, 63, 65, 70, 72, 74, 75, 76, 77, 78, 79, 83, 84, 85, 91, 92, 96, 97, 98, 99, 101, 103, 106, 113, 124, 126, 132, 140, 141, 142, 146, 147, 152, 153, 165, 176, 189

V

value-added tax (VAT), 27, 29, 30, 31, 38, 50, 51, 52, 53, 61, 63, 64, 65, 66, 67, 68, 69, 70, 71, 140, 156
values, 46, 47, 88, 89, 165
variability, 162
variable, 122
variation, 56, 151, 183
vehicles, 119
venture capital, 128
volatility, 167
voting, 128, 141

W

wage rate, 45
wages, 11, 14, 45, 49, 50, 51, 54, 55, 56, 87, 139
Wall Street Journal, 32
water, 65
water supplies, 66
weakness, 173
wealth, 46, 47
wear, 41
web, 11
welfare, 40
well-being, 143
wheat, 38
workers, ix, 1, 2, 3, 5, 8, 10, 11, 31, 46, 54, 82, 92, 143, 147, 174
World Bank, 142
WorldCom, 164

Y

yield, 52, 116